중학영어 **문법+쓰기**

STRUCTURE & FEATURES

중학 핵심 문법 30개를 활용한 체계적인 3단계 쓰기 훈련과 통합 서술형 문제 풀이로 문법과 쓰기를 연속으로 타파!

30개의 핵심 문법으로 문법 능력 충전

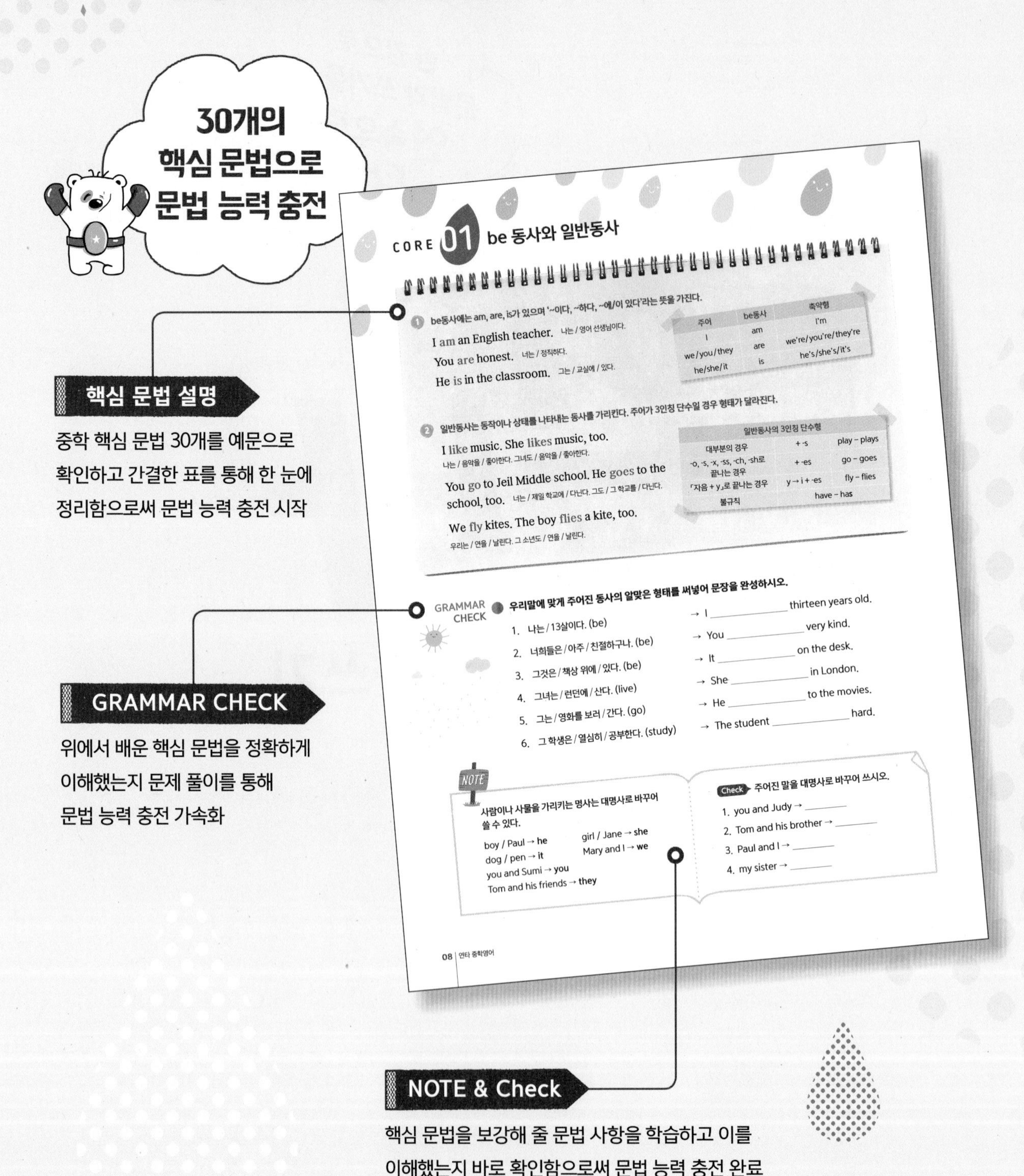

CORE 01 be 동사와 일반동사

① be동사에는 am, are, is가 있으며 '~이다, ~하다, ~에/이 있다'라는 뜻을 가진다.

I am an English teacher. 나는 / 영어 선생님이다.
You are honest. 너는 / 정직하다.
He is in the classroom. 그는 / 교실에 / 있다.

주어	be동사	축약형
I	am	I'm
we / you / they	are	we're/you're/they're
he/she/it	is	he's/she's/it's

② 일반동사는 동작이나 상태를 나타내는 동사를 가리킨다. 주어가 3인칭 단수일 경우 형태가 달라진다.

I like music. She likes music, too.
나는 / 음악을 / 좋아한다. 그녀도 / 음악을 / 좋아한다.

You go to Jeil Middle school. He goes to the school, too. 너는 / 제일 학교에 / 다닌다. 그도 / 그 학교를 / 다닌다.

We fly kites. The boy flies a kite, too.
우리는 / 연을 / 날린다. 그 소년도 / 연을 / 날린다.

일반동사의 3인칭 단수형		
대부분의 경우	+ -s	play – plays
-o, -s, -x, -ss, -ch, -sh로 끝나는 경우	+ -es	go – goes
「자음 + y」로 끝나는 경우	y → i + -es	fly – flies
불규칙		have – has

GRAMMAR CHECK 우리말에 맞게 주어진 동사의 알맞은 형태를 써넣어 문장을 완성하시오.

1. 나는 / 13살이다. (be) → I ______ thirteen years old.
2. 너희들은 / 아주 / 친절하구나. (be) → You ______ very kind.
3. 그것은 / 책상 위에 / 있다. (be) → It ______ on the desk.
4. 그녀는 / 런던에 / 산다. (live) → She ______ in London.
5. 그는 / 영화를 보러 / 간다. (go) → He ______ to the movies.
6. 그 학생은 / 열심히 / 공부한다. (study) → The student ______ hard.

NOTE
사람이나 사물을 가리키는 명사는 대명사로 바꾸어 쓸 수 있다.
boy / Paul → he
dog / pen → it
you and Sumi → you
Tom and his friends → they
girl / Jane → she
Mary and I → we

Check 주어진 말을 대명사로 바꾸어 쓰시오.
1. you and Judy → ______
2. Tom and his brother → ______
3. Paul and I → ______
4. my sister → ______

08 | 엔터 중학영어

핵심 문법 설명

중학 핵심 문법 30개를 예문으로 확인하고 간결한 표를 통해 한 눈에 정리함으로써 문법 능력 충전 시작

GRAMMAR CHECK

위에서 배운 핵심 문법을 정확하게 이해했는지 문제 풀이를 통해 문법 능력 충전 가속화

NOTE & Check

핵심 문법을 보강해 줄 문법 사항을 학습하고 이를 이해했는지 바로 확인함으로써 문법 능력 충전 완료

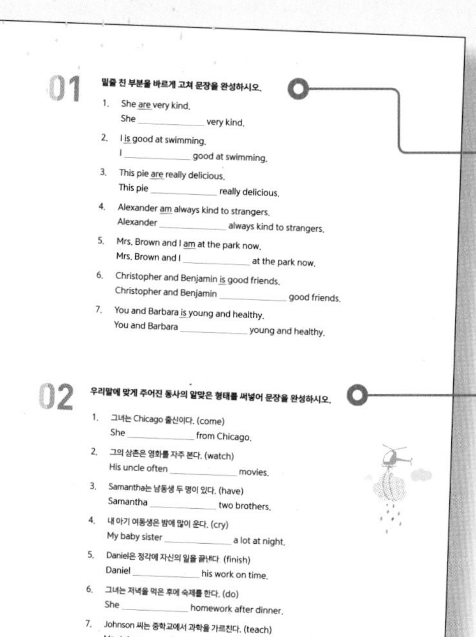

01 밑줄 친 부분을 바르게 고쳐 문장을 완성하시오.

1. She are very kind.
   She ________ very kind.
2. I is good at swimming.
   I ________ good at swimming.
3. This pie are really delicious.
   This pie ________ really delicious.
4. Alexander am always kind to strangers.
   Alexander ________ always kind to strangers.
5. Mrs. Brown and I am at the park now.
   Mrs. Brown and I ________ at the park now.
6. Christopher and Benjamin is good friends.
   Christopher and Benjamin ________ good friends.
7. You and Barbara is young and healthy.
   You and Barbara ________ young and healthy.

02 우리말에 맞게 주어진 동사의 알맞은 형태를 써넣어 문장을 완성하시오.

1. 그녀는 Chicago 출신이다. (come)
   She ________ from Chicago.
2. 그의 삼촌은 영화를 자주 본다. (watch)
   His uncle often ________ movies.
3. Samantha는 남동생 두 명이 있다. (have)
   Samantha ________ two brothers.
4. 내 아기 여동생은 밤에 많이 운다. (cry)
   My baby sister ________ a lot at night.
5. Daniel은 정각에 자신의 일을 끝낸다. (finish)
   Daniel ________ his work on time.
6. 그녀는 저녁을 먹은 후에 숙제를 한다. (do)
   She ________ homework after dinner.
7. Johnson 씨는 중학교에서 과학을 가르친다. (teach)
   Mr. Johnson ________ science at a middle school.

문법+쓰기, Chapter 01 | 09

도전 1단계

체계적인 단계별 쓰기 훈련의 첫 단계.
핵심 문법을 활용하여 틀리기 쉬운 부분을 확인해
가며 비교적 짧고 쉬운 단락 써보기

업그레이드 2단계

옮겨 쓰고 고쳐 쓰고 바꾸어 쓰는 훈련을 통해
자신감을 쌓고 문법과 쓰기를 동시에 Level Up

완성 3단계

1, 2단계 훈련을 바탕으로 어려운 문장과 통문장을
쓰면서 문법 및 문장 쓰기 능력 만렙 달성

03 Tina의 하루 일과표를 보고 내용과 일치하도록 문장을 완성하시오.

Tina's Daily Life

7:00 a.m. get up
7:30 a.m. have breakfast
8:00 a.m. go to school
4:00 p.m. practice piano
8:00 p.m. study Korean
10:30 p.m. write in her diary
11:30 p.m. go to bed

보기 Tina ____practices____ piano at 4 p.m.

Tina is a middle school student.
1. She ________ at 7 a.m.
2. She ________ at 7:30 a.m.
3. After breakfast she ________ at 8 a.m.
4. She ________ at 8 p.m.
5. She ________ before she goes to bed.

통합 서술형

그림을 보고 be동사와 주어진 단어를 사용하여 민호가 가족을 소개하는 글을 완성하시오.

My name ______ Minho. I have a large family.
My grandma ______ a good singer, and she often ______ funny songs. (sing)
My father ______ a doctor, and he ______ care of sick people. (take)
My mother ______ a teacher, and she ______ math at a high school. (teach)
My brother and I ______ students and we go to the same school.

10 | 연타 중학영어

다양한 유형의 통합 서술형 문제를
풀어봄으로써 통합적인 사고력과 문제 해결
능력을 향상시켜, 내신 서술형 평가 정복

Contents

CHAPTER 01

be동사와 일반동사

Core 01 | be동사와 일반동사 ···· 08

Core 02 | be동사 부정문과 일반동사 부정문 ···· 11

Core 03 | be동사 의문문과 일반동사 의문문 ···· 14

CHAPTER 02

시제

Core 04 | 과거시제 ···· 18

Core 05 | 미래시제 ···· 21

Core 06 | 진행시제 ···· 24

CHAPTER 03

조동사

Core 07 | can / may ···· 28

Core 08 | must / should ···· 31

CHAPTER 04

명사와 대명사

Core 09 | 셀 수 있는 명사와 셀 수 없는 명사 / There is(are) · 36

Core 10 | 셀 수 없는 명사의 수량 표현 ···· 39

Core 11 | 지시대명사 / 비인칭 주어 it ···· 42

Core 12 | 재귀대명사 ···· 45

Core 13 | 부정대명사 ···· 48

CHAPTER 05

형용사와 부사

Core 14 | 형용사와 부사 ···· 52

Core 15 | 수량 형용사 ···· 55

CHAPTER 06

비교

Core 16 | 형용사·부사의 비교급과 최상급 ······ 60
Core 17 | 비교급·최상급의 주요 표현 ······ 63
Core 18 | 원급의 주요 표현 ······ 66

CHAPTER 07

문장의 종류

Core 19 | 의문사가 있는 의문문 ······ 70
Core 20 | 명령문 / 권유문 / 감탄문 ······ 73
Core 21 | 부가의문문 / 선택의문문 ······ 76

CHAPTER 08

to부정사

Core 22 | 명사적 용법 ······ 80
Core 23 | 형용사적 용법 ······ 83
Core 24 | 부사적 용법 ······ 86

CHAPTER 09

동명사

Core 25 | 동명사의 역할 ······ 90
Core 26 | 동명사·to부정사를 목적어로 취하는 동사 ······ 93

CHAPTER 10

전치사와 접속사

Core 27 | 전치사 ······ 98
Core 28 | 등위접속사 ······ 101
Core 29 | 명사절을 이끄는 접속사 that ······ 104
Core 30 | 부사절을 이끄는 접속사 ······ 107

Chapter

01

be동사와 일반동사

CORE 01 be동사와 일반동사

CORE 02 be동사 부정문과 일반동사 부정문

CORE 03 be동사 의문문과 일반동사 의문문

CORE 01 be동사와 일반동사

1. be동사에는 am, are, is가 있으며 '~이다, ~하다, ~에/이 있다'라는 뜻을 가진다.

I **am** an English teacher. 나는 / 영어 선생님이다.

You **are** honest. 너는 / 정직하다.

He **is** in the classroom. 그는 / 교실에 / 있다.

주어	be동사	축약형
I	am	I'm
we/you/they	are	we're/you're/they're
he/she/it	is	he's/she's/it's

2. 일반동사는 동작이나 상태를 나타내는 동사를 가리킨다. 주어가 3인칭 단수일 경우 형태가 달라진다.

I **like** music. She **likes** music, too.
나는 / 음악을 / 좋아한다. 그녀도 / 음악을 / 좋아한다.

You **go** to Jeil Middle school. He **goes** to the school, too. 너는 / 제일 학교에 / 다닌다. 그도 / 그 학교를 / 다닌다.

We **fly** kites. The boy **flies** a kite, too.
우리는 / 연을 / 날린다. 그 소년도 / 연을 / 날린다.

일반동사의 3인칭 단수형		
대부분의 경우	+ -s	play – plays
-o, -s, -x, -ss, -ch, -sh로 끝나는 경우	+ -es	go – goes
「자음 + y」로 끝나는 경우	y → i + -es	fly – flies
불규칙	have – has	

GRAMMAR CHECK

우리말에 맞게 주어진 동사의 알맞은 형태를 써넣어 문장을 완성하시오.

1. 나는 / 13살이다. (be) → I ____________ thirteen years old.
2. 너희들은 / 아주 / 친절하구나. (be) → You ____________ very kind.
3. 그것은 / 책상 위에 / 있다. (be) → It ____________ on the desk.
4. 그녀는 / 런던에 / 산다. (live) → She ____________ in London.
5. 그는 / 영화를 보러 / 간다. (go) → He ____________ to the movies.
6. 그 학생은 / 열심히 / 공부한다. (study) → The student ____________ hard.

사람이나 사물을 가리키는 명사는 대명사로 바꾸어 쓸 수 있다.

boy / Paul → **he**
girl / Jane → **she**
dog / pen → **it**
Mary and I → **we**
you and Sumi → **you**
Tom and his friends → **they**

Check 주어진 말을 대명사로 바꾸어 쓰시오.

1. you and Judy → ________
2. Tom and his brother → ________
3. Paul and I → ________
4. my sister → ________

01 밑줄 친 부분을 바르게 고쳐 문장을 완성하시오.

1. She are very kind.
   She ______________ very kind.
2. I is good at swimming.
   I ______________ good at swimming.
3. This pie are really delicious.
   This pie ______________ really delicious.
4. Alexander am always kind to strangers.
   Alexander ______________ always kind to strangers.
5. Mrs. Brown and I am at the park now.
   Mrs. Brown and I ______________ at the park now.
6. Christopher and Benjamin is good friends.
   Christopher and Benjamin ______________ good friends.
7. You and Barbara is young and healthy.
   You and Barbara ______________ young and healthy.

02 우리말에 맞게 주어진 동사의 알맞은 형태를 써넣어 문장을 완성하시오.

1. 그녀는 Chicago 출신이다. (come)
   She ______________ from Chicago.
2. 그의 삼촌은 영화를 자주 본다. (watch)
   His uncle often ______________ movies.
3. Samantha는 남동생 두 명이 있다. (have)
   Samantha ______________ two brothers.
4. 내 아기 여동생은 밤에 많이 운다. (cry)
   My baby sister ______________ a lot at night.
5. Daniel은 정각에 자신의 일을 끝낸다. (finish)
   Daniel ______________ his work on time.
6. 그녀는 저녁을 먹은 후에 숙제를 한다. (do)
   She ______________ homework after dinner.
7. Johnson 씨는 중학교에서 과학을 가르친다. (teach)
   Mr. Johnson ______________ science at a middle school.

03 Tina의 하루 일과표를 보고 내용과 일치하도록 문장을 완성하시오.

7:00 a.m. get up
7:30 a.m. have breakfast
8:00 a.m. go to school

4:00 p.m. practice piano
8:00 p.m. study Korean
10:30 p.m. write in her diary
11:30 p.m. go to bed

보기 Tina ____practices____ piano at 4 p.m.

Tina is a middle school student.

1. She ______________________ at 7 a.m.
2. She ______________________ at 7:30 a.m.
3. After breakfast she ______________________ at 8 a.m.
4. She ______________________ at 8 p.m.
5. She ______________________ before she goes to bed.

통합 서술형

그림을 보고 be동사와 주어진 단어를 사용하여 민호가 가족을 소개하는 글을 완성하시오.

My name ________ Minho. I have a large family.

My grandma ________ a good singer, and she often ________ funny songs. (sing)

My father ________ a doctor, and he ________ care of sick people. (take)

My mother ________ a teacher, and she ________ math at a high school. (teach)

My brother and I ________ students and we go to the same school.

CORE 02 be동사 부정문과 일반동사 부정문

1. be동사의 부정문은 be동사 뒤에 not을 쓰며, '~이 아니다, ~하지 않다, ~에/이 없다'라는 뜻이다.

I **am not** Canadian. 나는 / 캐나다 사람이 / 아니다.

You **are not** happy. 너는 / 행복하지 / 않다.

The students **are not** in the classroom.
학생들은 / 교실에 / 없다.

주어	be동사	축약형
I	am not	X
we/you/they	are not	aren't
he/she/it	is not	isn't

2. 일반동사의 부정문은 일반동사의 원형 앞에 「do/does not」을 쓰며, '~하지 않는다'라는 뜻이 된다.

We **do not like** cold weather.
우리는 / 추운 날씨를 / 좋아하지 / 않는다.

He **does not play** the piano at night.
그는 / 밤에는 / 피아노를 / 치지 / 않는다.

주어	일반동사 부정형	축약형
I/we/you/they	do not	don't
he/she/it	does not	doesn't

GRAMMAR CHECK

다음 문장을 부정문으로 바꾸어 쓰시오.

1. It is delicious. 그것은 맛있다.
____
2. We are hungry now. 우리는 지금 배고프다.
____
3. They get up early. 그들은 일찍 일어난다.
____
4. James knows the answer. James는 정답을 알고 있다.
____
5. He is a member of the club. 그는 그 클럽의 회원이다.
____
6. She likes sandwiches. 그녀는 샌드위치를 좋아한다.
____
7. The dog and the cat are on the bed. 그 개와 고양이는 침대 위에 있다.
____

01

틀린 부분을 바르게 고쳐 문장을 다시 쓰시오.

1. Not I am busy today.

   ____

2. They does not play computer games.

   ____

3. This story aren't funny to me.

   ____

4. You do understand not my feelings.

   ____

5. Her uncle doesn't goes to the beach.

   ____

6. Elizabeth don't likes meat or fish.

   ____

02

주어진 단어를 사용하여 우리말에 맞게 문장을 완성하시오.

1. 오늘 날씨가 춥지 않다. (be, cold)

   The weather ______________________________ today.

2. 너는 이제 나의 이웃이 아니다. (be, my neighbor)

   ______________________________ now.

3. 그는 숲에서 곰을 사냥하지 않는다. (hunt)

   ______________________________ bears in the forest.

4. 내 여동생은 컴퓨터로 만화영화를 보지 않는다. (watch cartoons)

   ______________________________ on her computer.

5. Jane과 나는 지금 야구장에 있지 않다. (be, at the ballpark)

   ______________________________ now.

6. Bill과 그의 형은 클래식 음악을 듣지 않는다 (listen to)

   ______________________________ classical music.

03 나와 Susan에 대한 그림을 보고 <보기>와 같이 문장을 완성하시오.

보기

Susan wears a cap. I wear a hat.
I ___don't wear___ a cap.

1.

I play the piano. Susan plays the violin.
She ______________ the piano.

2.

Susan is tall.
I ______________ tall.

3.

I have a dog. Susan has a cat.
She ______________ a dog.

통합서술형

● 표를 보고 <보기>와 같이 문장을 완성하시오.

	O	X
Ms. Thompson	a teacher	a student
John	play soccer	play basketball
the children	drink juice	drink coffee
Kate and Sam	13 years old	15 years old
Jane's mom	wash the dishes	clean the windows
Alice and I	like history	like math

보기 Ms. Thompson is a teacher. She ___is not___ a student.

1. John plays soccer. He ______________ basketball.
2. The children drink juice. They ______________ coffee.
3. Kate and Sam are 13 years old. ______________ 15 years old.
4. Jane's mom washes the dishes. ______________ clean the windows.
5. Alice and I like history. ______________ math.

CORE 03 be동사 의문문과 일반동사 의문문

① be동사 의문문은 be동사를 주어 앞에 써 「be동사+주어 ~?」 형태로 나타내며, Yes/No로 대답한다.

Am I wrong? - Yes, you are.
제가 / 틀렸나요? - 네, 틀렸어요.

Are you in my class? - No, I'm not.
너는 / 우리 / 반이니? - 아니, 그렇지 / 않아.

Is he kind? - Yes, he is.
그는 / 친절하니? - 그래, 친절해.

be동사 의문문	대답
Am I ~?	Yes, 주어+be동사. No, 주어+be동사+not.
Are you/we/they ~?	
Is he/she/it ~?	

② 일반동사 의문문은 주어 앞에 Do/Does를 써서 「Do/Does+주어+동사원형 ~?」 형태로 나타내며, Yes/No로 대답한다.

Do you like the song?
- Yes, we do.
너희들은 / 그 노래를 / 좋아하니? - 네, 좋아해요.

Does she live here?
- No, she doesn't.
그녀는 / 여기에 / 사나요? - 아니오, 여기에 / 살지 / 않아요.

일반동사 의문문	대답
Do I+동사원형 ~?	Yes, you+do. / No, you+don't.
Do you/we/they + 동사원형 ~?	Yes, 주어+do. / No, 주어+don't.
Does he/she/it + 동사원형 ~?	Yes, 주어+does. / No, 주어+doesn't.

GRAMMAR CHECK

다음 문장을 의문문으로 바꾸어 쓰시오.

1. You are tired. 너는 피곤하다.

____

2. The car is expensive. 그 차는 비싸다.

____

3. They go to the museum. 그들은 박물관에 간다.

____

4. We need a pet. 우리는 애완동물이 필요하다.

____

5. I am late for school. 내가 수업에 늦었다.

____

6. He speaks French well. 그는 프랑스어를 잘한다.

____

01

주어진 단어를 사용하여 우리말에 맞게 문장을 완성하시오.

1. 너는 중학생이니? (a middle school student)
   ____

2. Brown 씨는 의사인가요? (a doctor, Mr. Brown)
   ____

3. Tom과 Mary는 같은 반이니? (Tom and Mary)
   ______________________________ in the same class?

4. 너는 방과 후에 중국어를 배우니? (learn Chinese)
   ______________________________ after school?

5. 그는 일요일마다 영화를 보러 가나요? (go to the movies)
   ______________________________ every Sunday?

6. Annie는 지금 휴대전화를 가지고 있니? (have a cell phone)
   ______________________________ now?

02

<보기>와 같이 우리말에 맞게 대화를 완성하시오.

보기 A: Is the game exciting? 그 경기는 흥미진진하니?
B: ____Yes, it is.____ 응, 흥미진진해.

1. A: Are you John's friend? 너는 John의 친구니?
   B: ______________________________ 응, 친구야.

2. A: Does she exercise every day? 그녀는 매일 운동하니?
   B: ______________________________ 아니, 하지 않아.

3. A: ______________________________ 그 가방은 비싼가요?
   B: No, it isn't. 아뇨, 비싸지 않아요.

4. A: ______________________________ 너는 우유를 마시니?
   B: Yes, I do. 응, 그래.

5. A: ______________________________ 내가 수업에 늦었니?
   B: ______________________________ 응, 늦었어.

6. A: ______________________________ Andy는 수학을 가르치나요?
   B: ______________________________ 아뇨, 그렇지 않습니다.

03 틀린 부분을 바르게 고쳐 문장을 다시 쓰시오.

1.

A: Do she likes roses?

____

B: Yes, she does.

2.

A: Does Paul a farmer?

____

B: Yes, he is.

3.

A: Are David and Clara firefighters?

B: No, they isn't.

____

4.

A: Do you teach history?

B: No, you don't.

____

통합 서술형

Bill과 Jack을 소개한 표를 보고 아래 대화를 완성하시오.

이름	Bill	Jack
나이	13 yeas old	14 years
사는 곳	Chicago	Miami
좋아하는 것	basketball	surfing

1. Kate: ________ your name Jack?
   Bill: No, ________ ________. My name is Bill.

2. Kate: ________ ________ 13 years old?
   Bill: Yes, ________ ________.
   Kate: How about you, Jack? ________ ________ 13 years old, too?
   Jack: ________, I ________ ________. I am 14 years old.

3. Kate: ________ ________ live in Miami?
   Jack: Yes, ________ ________. And I like surfing.
   Kate: Bill, ________ ________ like surfing?
   Bill: ________, ________ ________. I like basketball.

Chapter 02

시제

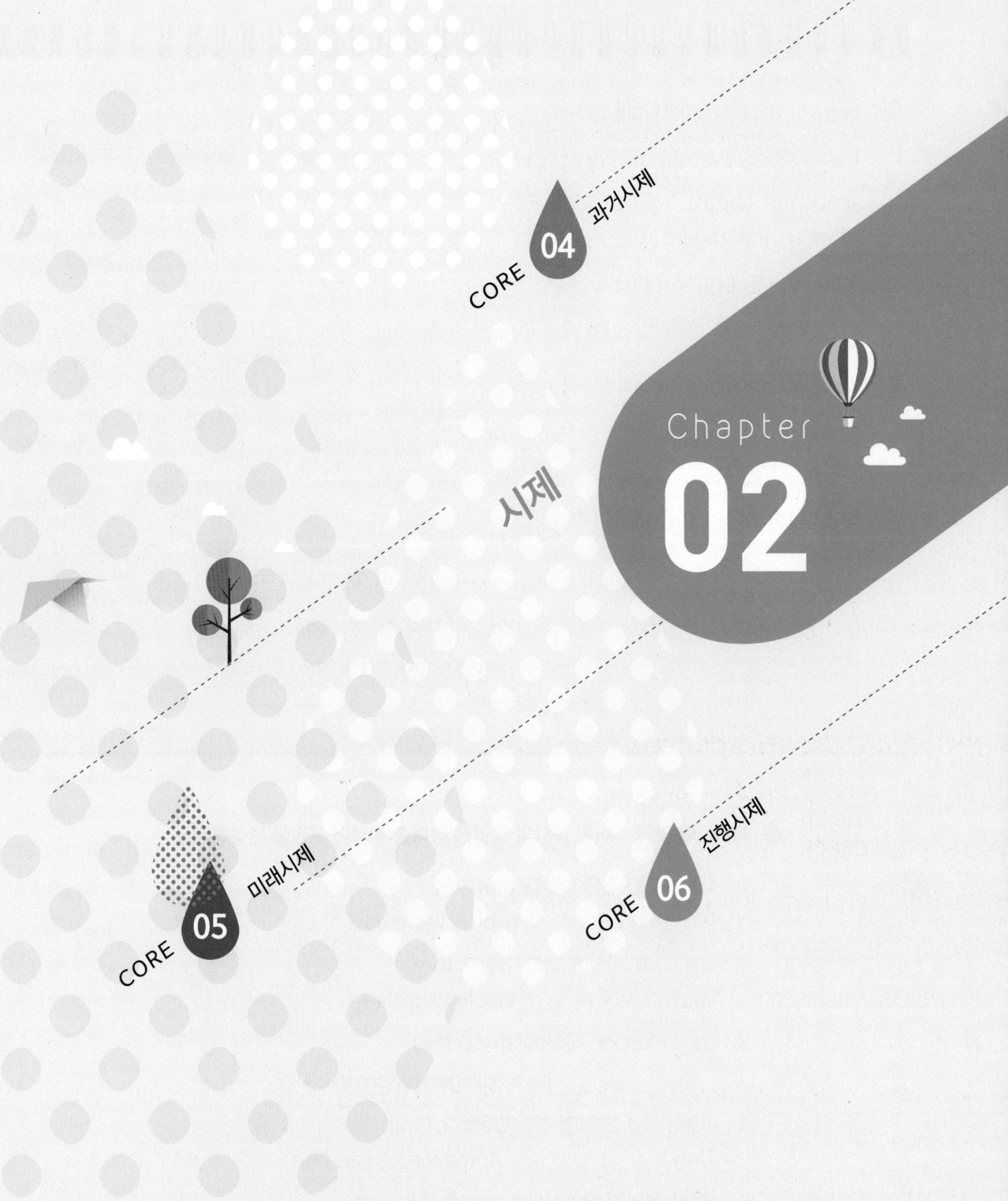

CORE 04 과거시제

① be동사의 과거시제: 과거의 상태를 나타낸다.

I **was** sick yesterday. So my parents **were not** happy. 나는 / 어제 / 아팠다. 그래서 / 부모님께서는 / 즐겁지 / 않으셨다.

Was she in London last week?
그녀는 / 지난주에 / 런던에 / 있었나요?

동사 형태	부정문	의문문
am/is → was are → were	was/were +not	Was/Were+주어 ~? – Yes, 주어+was/were. – No, 주어+wasn't/weren't.

② 일반동사의 과거시제: 과거에 이미 끝난 일을 나타낸다.

I **studied** last night.
나는 / 어젯밤에 / 공부했다.

But my brother **didn't study**.
그러나 / 형은 / 공부하지 / 않았다.

Did you **play** baseball?
너는 / 야구를 / 했니?

동사 형태	규칙 변화	대부분의 동사: +-ed	play → played
		-e로 끝나는 동사: +-d	like → liked
		「자음+y」로 끝나는 동사: y → i+-ed	study → studied
		「단모음+단자음」으로 끝나는 동사: 자음+-ed	plan → planned
	불규칙 변화	buy → bought come → came do → did have → had go → went make → made read→ read send → sent sing → sang	
부정문	did not(didn't)+동사원형		
의문문	Did+주어+동사원형 ~? – Yes, 주어+did. / No, 주어+didn't.		

GRAMMAR CHECK ◐ **우리말에 맞게 주어진 동사의 알맞은 형태를 써넣어 문장을 완성하시오.**

1. 나는 / 어제 / 아주 / 바빴다. (be)
   I ______________ very busy yesterday.
2. 너는 / 그때 / 파리에 / 있지 / 않았다. (be)
   You ______________ not in Paris then.
3. 그는 / 2002년에 / 대학생이었나요? (be)
   ______________ he a college student in 2002?
4. 그들은 / 3년 전에 / 한국을 / 방문했다. (visit)
   They ______________ Korea three years ago.
5. 내 여동생은 / 지난 토요일에 / 숙제를 / 했다. (do)
   My little sister ______________ her homework last Saturday.
6. Emily와 Jim은 / 작년에 / 내 생일 파티에 / 왔다. (come)
   Emily and Jim ______________ to my birthday party last year.

01

다음 문장을 지시대로 바꾸어 쓰시오.

1. She is my English teacher. (과거시제)

____

2. We are interested in the news. (과거시제)

____

3. The history class is boring. (과거시제 부정문)

____

4. Are Kate and Jane your friends? (과거시제)

____

5. You are at the library. (과거시제 의문문)

____

02

주어진 단어를 사용하여 우리말에 맞게 문장을 완성하시오

1. 그는 Jane의 생일 파티 계획을 세웠다. (plan)

______________________ for Jane's birthday party.

2. 나는 지난 주말에 세차하지 않았다. (wash)

______________________ the car last weekend.

3. 그들은 2010년에 그 질병을 연구했다. (study, the disease)

______________________ in 2010.

4. 그 문은 지난 밤에 닫혔나요? (close, the door)

______________________ last night?

5. 그녀는 John에게 줄 선물을 샀다. (buy, the gift)

______________________ for John.

6. Jonathan은 한 시간 전에 아침을 먹었다. (have, breakfast)

______________________ an hour ago.

7. 우리는 어제 아이들을 위해 인형을 만들었다. (make, dolls)

______________________ for the kids yesterday.

03 Paul의 체크 리스트를 보고 아래 문장을 완성하시오.

What did Paul do last Sunday?	
read a book	V
visit his grandparents	
1. go shopping	V
2. play basketball with his friends	
3. send an e-mail to Mary	V
4. clean his room	
5. make sandwiches for his family	V

보기 Paul ______ read a book ______ last Sunday.
He ______ didn't visit his grandparents ______ last Sunday.

1. He ______________________ last Sunday.
2. He ______________________ last Sunday.
3. He ______________________ last Sunday.
4. He ______________________ last Sunday.
5. He ______________________ last Sunday.

통합 서술형

◎ 다음은 Eva의 일기이다. 주어진 단어를 사용하여 일기를 완성하시오.

Yesterday, I went to the hospital with my music club members.
We ____________ a concert for sick children. (give)
Tom ____________ the guitar and Edward ____________ the drums. (play)
I ____________ anything. (not, play) I ____________ songs. (sing)
It ____________ an exciting concert. (be) Everybody ____________ fun. (have)

CORE 05 미래시제

1 will을 사용한 미래 표현: 앞으로 일어날 일을 나타낸다.

I **will watch** the movie. But he **will not watch** it.
나는 / 그 영화를 / 볼 것이다. 그러나 / 그는 / 보지 / 않을 것이다.

Will Bill **help** you with your homework?
Bill이 / 네 숙제를 / 도와줄 거니?

* 미래를 나타내는 부사(구): tomorrow, next week, next month, next year, in 2080

긍정문	will+동사원형
부정문	will not(won't)
의문문	Will+주어+동사원형 ~? – Yes, 주어+will – No, 주어+won't.

2 be going to를 사용한 미래 표현: 가까운 미래의 계획을 나타낸다.

I **am going to meet** Jim next week. But she **is not going to meet** him.
그는 / 다음 주에 / Jim을 / 만날 예정이다. 그러나 / 그녀는 / 그를 / 만나지 / 않을 예정이다.

Are you **going to visit** England?
당신은 / 영국을 / 방문할 / 계획인가요?

긍정문	I am going to+동사원형 You/We/They are going to+동사원형 He/She/It is going to+동사원형
부정문	am/are/is+not+going to
의문문	Am/Are/Is+주어+going to ~? – Yes, 주어+am/are/is. – No, 주어+am/are/is+not.

GRAMMAR CHECK

우리말에 맞게 주어진 동사의 알맞은 형태를 써넣어 문장을 완성하시오.

1. 너는 / 곧 / 정답을 / 알게 될 것이다. (know)
   You ______ ______ the answer soon.
2. 나는 / 내일 / 사진을 / 찍을 예정이다. (take)
   I ______ ______ ______ ______ pictures tomorrow.
3. 그 잎들은 / 바람에 / 떨어지지 / 않을 것이다. (fall)
   The leaves ______ ______ ______ in the wind.
4. 오늘 밤에 / 우리 집에 / 올 거니? (come)
   ______ you ______ to my home tonight?
5. 그 상점은 / 오늘 오후에는 / 문을 열지 / 않을 예정이다. (open)
   The store ______ ______ ______ ______ ______ this afternoon.

01

다음 문장을 지시대로 바꾸어 쓰시오.

1. I am a nurse. (미래시제)

   ____

2. We write a letter to Bill. (미래시제 부정문)

   ____

3. You clean the windows. (미래시제 의문문)

   ____

4. The class is going to start soon. (부정문)

   ____

5. Robin's brother is going to leave for London this evening. (의문문)

   ____

02

다음 새해 계획표와 내용이 일치하도록 문장을 완성하시오.

Mike
- 10 years old
- Get up early in the morning
- Not play computer games

1. Mike will be 10 years old next year.

   He is going to get up early in the morning.

   He ______________________________ .

Judy
- 14 years old
- Study hard
- Not be late for school

2. Judy ______________________________ .

   She ______________________________ .

   She ______________________________ .

Dad
- 40 years old
- Not eat hamburgers
- Be kind to his neighbors

3. ______________________________

   ____

   ____

03 주어진 단어를 사용하여 우리말에 맞게 문장을 완성하시오.

1. 나는 내일 아침에 조깅을 할 계획이다. (going, jog)

   ______________________________ tomorrow morning.

2. Ted는 오늘 오후에 그 집을 방문할 것이다. (will)

   ______________________________ this afternoon.

3. 그 기차는 5시에 떠나지 않을 예정이다. (going, leave)

   ______________________________ at 5.

4. 그는 이번 여름에 역사를 공부하나요? (will)

   ______________________________ this summer?

5. Allan과 Ed는 7시까지 그 일을 끝낼 계획이다. (going, finish)

   ______________________________ by 7 o'clock.

6. 그녀는 내일 엄마를 도와드릴 건가요? (will)

   ______________________________ tomorrow?

통합 서술형

Rainbow 학교 축제 안내문을 보고 축제를 소개하는 글을 완성하시오.

Rainbow School Festival	
May 7	Have a festival
10:30 a.m.	Make a speech
11:30 a.m.	Play music (school band)
12:30 p.m.	Have lunch
2:00 p.m.	Play *Snow White* (drama club)
4:30 p.m.	Hold a dance party

Rainbow School will have a festival on May 7.

(1) Mr. Smith ______________________ at 10:30.

(2) After the speech, the school band ______________________.

(3) At 12:30, we ______________________.

(4) After lunch, the drama club ______________________.

(5) We ______________________ at 4:30.

Would you come to Rainbow School Festival?

CORE 06 진행시제

① 현재진행시제: '~하고 있다'라는 뜻으로 현재 진행 중인 일을 나타낸다.

I **am eating** an apple and a sandwich.
But he **is not eating** anything.
나는 / 사과와 샌드위치를 / 먹고 있다. 그러나 / 그는 / 아무것도 / 먹고 있지 않다.

Are you **talking** to your friends?
너는 / 친구들과 / 이야기하고 있니?

긍정문	am/are/is+동사-ing
부정문	am/are/is+not+동사-ing
의문문	Am/Are/Is+주어+동사-ing ~? - Yes, 주어+am/are/is. - No, 주어+am/are/is+not.

② 과거진행시제: '~하고 있었다'라는 뜻으로 과거 진행 중이었던 일을 나타낸다.

I **was doing** my homework then.
나는 / 그때 / 숙제를 / 하고 있었다.

Were you **playing** outside?
너는 / 밖에서 / 놀고 있었니?

긍정문	was/were+동사-ing
부정문	was/were+not+동사-ing
의문문	Was/Were+주어+동사-ing ~? - Yes, 주어+was/were. - No, 주어+was/were+not.

GRAMMAR CHECK

다음 문장을 지시대로 바꾸어 쓰시오.

1. I read a novel. (현재진행)

____

2. He cooked in the kitchen. (과거진행)

____

3. They were learning Japanese then. (부정문)

____

4. You were cleaning your room at that time. (의문문)

____

NOTE

동사의 -ing형 만들기

대부분의 동사	+ -ing	sing → singing
-e로 끝나는 동사	-e 빼고 + -ing	come → coming
「단모음+단자음」으로 끝나는 동사	자음 추가 + -ing	sit → sitting
-ie로 끝나는 동사	ie → y + -ing	lie → lying

Check 다음 동사의 -ing형을 쓰시오.

1. come → ____________
2. have → ____________
3. run → ____________
4. tie → ____________

01 우리말에 맞게 주어진 동사의 알맞은 형태를 써넣어 문장을 완성하시오.

1. 그는 공원에서 자전거를 타고 있다. (ride)

   He ______ ______ a bike in the park.

2. 나는 전화 통화를 하고 있지 않다. (talk)

   I ______ ______ ______ on the phone.

3. 너는 지금 의자에 앉아 있니? (sit)

   ______ you ______ on the chair now?

4. Jane은 고양이 목에 방울을 달고 있었다. (tie)

   Jane ______ ______ a bell onto the cat.

5. 그들은 그때 책상을 옮기고 있었나요? (move)

   ______ they ______ the desk then?

6. Bill과 그의 친구들은 강에서 수영을 하고 있지 않았다. (swim)

   Bill and his friends ______ ______ ______ in the river.

02 틀린 부분을 바르게 고쳐 문장을 다시 쓰시오.

1. She making pasta now.

   ____

2. Sam not is going to the market.

   ____

3. Were he using a fax at that time?

   ____

4. He and I was solving math problems.

   ____

5. Do you lying on the sofa now?

   ____

6. You and your sister was shopping at the mall.

   ____

03 주어진 단어를 사용하여 우리말에 맞게 문장을 쓰시오.

1.

그는 지금 쇼핑을 하고 있다. (shop)

____

2.

너는 편지를 쓰고 있었니? (write a letter)

____

3.

Tom과 Amy는 야외에서 뛰고 있다. (run, outdoors)

____

4.

그 고양이는 소파에 누워 있지 않았다. (lie, on the sofa)

____

통합 서술형

◎ 주어진 단어를 사용하여 그림을 설명하는 글을 완성하시오.

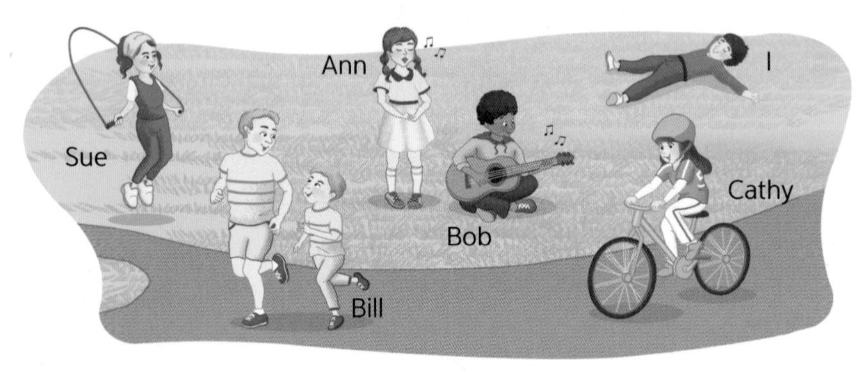

My friends and I are in the park now.

Sue ______________ rope, and Bill ______________ with his father.

Ann ______________ a song, and Bob ______________ the guitar.

Cathy ______________ a bike, and I ______________ on the grass.

We ______________ a good time in the park!

play	have	sing	ride	lie	jog	jump

Chapter 03

조동사

CORE 07 can / may

CORE 08 must / should

CORE 07 can / may

1 조동사 can은 능력, 허락, 요청을 나타낸다.

I **can** speak Chinese. (= am able to) <능력>
나는 / 중국어를 / 말할 수 있다.

You **can** visit me anytime. <허락>
너는 / 언제든 / 나를 / 찾아와도 된다.

Can you do me a favor? <요청>
제 부탁 하나만 / 들어주시겠습니까?

긍정문	can+동사원형
부정문	cannot(can't)+동사원형
의문문	Can+주어+동사원형? - Yes, 주어+can. - No, 주어+can't.

2 조동사 may는 허락, 추측을 나타낸다.

May I use your pen? (= can) <허락>
제가 / 당신의 펜을 / 사용해도 되나요?

She **may** not know the truth. <추측>
그녀는 / 진실을 / 알지 못할지도 모른다.

긍정문	may+동사원형
부정문	may not+동사원형
의문문	May+주어+동사원형? - Yes, 주어+may. - No, 주어+may not.

GRAMMAR CHECK

틀린 부분을 바르게 고쳐 문장을 다시 쓰시오.

1. A giraffe can runs very fast.

____

2. The work mays be very difficult for you.

____

3. The team doesn't can play tomorrow.

____

4. Are you able move this furniture?

____

5. May ask I a question?

____

6. They may be not at home at this time.

____

01

우리말에 맞게 빈칸에 알맞은 말을 쓰시오.

1. 나는 매우 높이 뛸 수 있다.
   I ________________ jump very high.

2. 이 장난감은 아이들에게 위험할지도 모른다.
   This toy ________________ be dangerous for kids.

3. 네가 내일 나에게 전화해 줄래?
   ________________ you call me tomorrow?

4. 제가 질문 하나 해도 될까요?
   ________________ I ask a question?

5. 그녀는 스테이크를 요리할 수 있다.
   She __________ __________ __________ cook steak.

6. 너는 한 달 후에 그 편지를 열어 봐도 된다.
   You ________________ open the letter in a month.

02

주어진 단어를 사용하여 우리말에 맞게 문장을 완성하시오.

1. 그녀가 대회에서 우승할지도 모른다. (win)
   ________________________________ the contest.

2. 우리는 답을 찾아낼 수 없다. (find)
   ________________________________ the answer.

3. 그 아기는 이제 일어설 수 있다. (able, stand up)
   ________________________________ now.

4. 너는 Evan을 우리 모임에 초대해도 된다. (invite)
   ________________________________ to our meeting.

5. 여기서 그를 기다려 주시겠어요? (wait for)
   ________________________________ here?

6. 제가 당신의 여권을 봐도 될까요? (see)
   ________________________________ your passport?

7. Sally와 Tim이 그 과학자를 만나지 못할지도 모른다. (meet)
   ________________________________ the scientist.

03 주어진 단어를 사용하여 우리말에 맞게 문장을 완성하시오.

1. 

창문을 열어 주시겠어요? (the window)

____

2. 

그녀는 그 차를 고칠 수 있다. (repair)

____

3. 

제가 당신과 춤을 춰도 될까요? (dance with)

____

4. 

여기서는 소리내어 읽어서는 안 됩니다. (read aloud)

____

통합서술형

친구들에 대한 표를 보고 아래 글을 완성하시오.

	David	Sara	Paul
speak Spanish	O	O	X
play the piano	X	O	O
eat with chopsticks	O	X	O
ride a skateboard	O	O	X

I have three good friends.

David can speak Spanish but Paul can't speak Spanish.

(1) Sara ________ the piano but David ________________ the piano.

(2) Paul ________ with chopsticks but Sara ________________ with chopsticks.

(3) David ________ a skateboard but Paul ________________ a skateboard.

CORE 08 must / should

1 조동사 must는 강제적 의무, 강한 추측을 나타낸다.

Passengers **must** wear seat belts. (= have to)

<강제적 의무> 승객들은 / 안전벨트를 / 매야 한다.

She **must** be happy. <강한 추측> 그녀는 / 기쁜 것이 / 틀림없다.

You **must not** park here. <강한 금지>

당신은 / 여기에 / 주차하면 / 안 됩니다.

You **don't have to** go there. (= don't need to)

<불필요> 너는 / 거기에 / 갈 필요가 없다.

긍정문	must+동사원형 = have/has to+동사원형
부정문	must not(mustn't)+동사원형 (강한 금지) ≠ don't/doesn't have(need) to +동사원형 (불필요)
의문문	Must+주어+동사원형? = Do/Does+주어+have to+동사원형?

2 조동사 should는 도덕적 의무, 충고를 나타낸다.

We **should** respect elderly people. (= ought to)

<의무・충고> 우리는 / 노인을 / 공경해야 한다.

You **should not** ignore people. (= ought not to)

<금지> 너는 / 사람들을 / 무시하면 / 안 된다.

긍정문	should+동사원형 = ought to+동사원형
부정문	should not(shouldn't)+동사원형 (금지) = ought not to+동사원형
의문문	Should+주어+동사원형?

GRAMMAR CHECK

밑줄 친 부분에 유의하여 두 문장의 의미가 같도록 빈칸을 채우시오.

1. Drivers must have a driver's license.
   = Drivers ______ ______ have a driver's license.

2. You should be kind to children.
   = You ______ ______ be kind to children.

3. Must we bring our lunch?
   = ______ we ______ ______ bring our lunch?

4. You ought not to skip your classes.
   = You ______ ______ skip your classes.

5. They don't need to finish the work.
   = They ______ ______ ______ finish the work.

01 틀린 부분을 바르게 고쳐 문장을 다시 쓰시오.

1. He ought make dinner today.

   ____

2. My brother have to prepare for the exam.

   ____

3. We don't must break the law.

   ____

4. Does she should answer the question?

   ____

5. You have not to get up early tomorrow.

   ____

6. Do Jessica has to wear glasses?

   ____

02 주어진 단어를 사용하여 우리말에 맞게 문장을 완성하시오.

1. 학생들은 교실을 나가면 안 된다. (must, leave)

   ______________________________ the classroom.

2. 너는 저녁 8시까지 집으로 와야 한다. (ought, come)

   ______________________________ home by 8 p.m.

3. 그는 그 소식에 놀란 것이 틀림없다. (surprised)

   ______________________________ at the news.

4. Sally는 따뜻한 옷을 가져와야 하나요? (have, bring)

   ______________________________ warm clothes?

5. 그녀는 그 병원의 의사임이 틀림없다. (a doctor)

   ______________________________ at the hospital.

6. Steve는 잔디를 깎을 필요가 없다. (mow)

   ______________________________ the lawn.

03 주어진 단어를 사용하여 우리말에 맞게 문장을 완성하시오.

1.

우리는 이 벽을 칠해야 하나요? (should, this wall)

____

2.

그녀는 수학 교사임이 틀림없다. (a math teacher)

____

3.

우리는 음식을 낭비하면 안 된다. (should, waste)

____

4.

Ann은 그 약을 먹을 필요가 없다. (take the medicine)

____

통합서술형

● 주어진 단어를 사용하여 표지판과 일치하도록 문장을 완성하시오.

Employees must wash their hands.

You must not(mustn't) smoke here.

1. Passengers ______________________ their seat belts.

2. Visitors ______________________ pictures here.

3. People ______________________ life jackets.

4. You ______________________ in this river.

wear	take	fasten	swim

Chapter
04
명사와 대명사
CORE 09 셀 수 있는 명사와 셀 수 없는 명사 / There is(are)
CORE 10 셀 수 없는 명사의 수량 표현
CORE 11 지시대명사 / 비인칭 주어 it
CORE 12 재귀대명사
CORE 13 부정대명사

CORE 09 셀 수 있는 명사와 셀 수 없는 명사 / There is(are)

① 셀 수 있는 명사: 하나일 때는 앞에 a(n)을 쓰고, 둘 이상일 때는 복수형을 쓴다.

I have a pen and two pencils.
나는 / 펜 한 개와 / 연필 두 자루를 / 가지고 있다.

He moved three boxes.
그는 / 상자 세 개를 / 옮겼다.

셀 수 있는 명사의 복수형	
대부분의 명사: +-s	cap → caps
-(s)s, -x, -o, -ch, -sh로 끝나면: +-es	bench → benches
「자음+y」로 끝나면: y→i+-es	baby → babies
-f/-fe로 끝나면: f(e)→v+-es	leaf → leaves

② 셀 수 없는 명사: 앞에 a(n)을 쓸 수 없고, 항상 단수형으로 쓴다.

Love is the most important thing.
사랑은 / 가장 중요한 / 것이다.

They want to drink water.
그들은 / 물을 / 마시기를 원한다.

셀 수 없는 명사
love, beauty, peace, life, advice, luck water, salt, bread, juice, money, hair Jane, Seoul, England, Monday ...

③ There is(are): '~이 있다'라는 뜻으로, 「There is+단수명사」, 「There are+복수명사」의 형태로 쓴다.

There is a tree, but there aren't any flowers. 나무는 / 한 그루 있지만, 꽃들은 / 전혀 없다.

GRAMMAR CHECK 둘 중에서 어법에 맞는 것을 고르시오.

1. I saw four (elephant / elephants) at the zoo.
2. There aren't any tall (building / buildings) in this city.
3. Put (salt / salts) in the chicken soup.
4. My brother bought (car / a car) yesterday.
5. The teacher gave me (advice / an advice).
6. Tommy received a letter from (a Jane / Jane).

셀 수 있는 명사의 불규칙 복수형

tooth → teeth　goose → geese　foot → feet
man → men　woman → women　child → children

cf. 단수형과 복수형의 형태가 같은 명사
fish → fish　sheep → sheep　deer → deer

Check 다음 명사의 복수형을 쓰시오.

1. tooth → ________
2. fish → ________
3. woman → ________

01

주어진 단어의 알맞은 형태를 써넣어 문장을 완성하시오.

1. Christine washed many ____________ . (dish)
2. The couple has two ____________ . (baby)
3. Five ____________ shouted in the restaurant. (man)
4. Ten ____________ are waiting for passengers. (bus)
5. Did you get ten ____________ from the farmer? (potato)
6. I saw many ____________ on the street. (leaf)
7. Look at the small ____________ of the boy. (foot)
8. Find empty ____________ in the park. (bench)
9. She borrowed six ____________ from me. (knife)
10. There are eight ____________ on the lake. (goose)

02

우리말에 맞게 틀린 부분을 바르게 고쳐 문장을 다시 쓰시오.

1. My sister has red hairs. 내 여동생은 빨간 머리이다.

   ____

2. We ate breads for lunch. 우리는 점심으로 빵을 먹었다.

   ____

3. Ashley teaches childs at a preschool. Ashley는 유치원에서 어린이들을 가르친다.

   ____

4. There is some books on the desk. 책상 위에 몇 권의 책들이 있다.

   ____

5. Jason finished five story. Jason은 5편의 이야기들을 완성했다.

   ____

6. She put some moneys into her account. 그녀는 자신의 계좌에 약간의 돈을 넣었다.

   ____

7. He told us his opinion on a life. 그는 인생에 대한 그의 의견을 말했다.

   ____

03 주어진 단어를 사용하여 우리말에 맞게 문장을 완성하시오.

1.

공원에 네 명의 어린이들이 있다. (child)

_______________ at the park.

2.

잔디 위에 벤치 하나가 있다. (bench)

_______________ on the grass.

3.

우리들은 나뭇잎들과 꽃들을 본다. (leaf, flower)

We see _______________ .

4.

사람들은 샌드위치들과 주스를 즐긴다. (sandwich, juice)

People enjoy _______________ .

통합 서술형

● 주어진 단어를 사용하여 우리말에 맞게 아래 글을 완성하시오.

William의 친구들은 그를 위해서 생일파티를 열 것이다.
Anna는 준비할 것이다.
Tim은  살 것이다.
Karen은  가져올 것이다.
모두가 즐거운 시간을 보낼 것이다.

William's friends will throw a birthday party for him.

Anna will _______________ .

Tim _______________ .

Karen _______________ .

Everybody will have a wonderful time.

buy	bring	prepare

CORE 10 셀 수 없는 명사의 수량 표현

● 셀 수 없는 명사는 담는 용기나 단위를 이용하여 수량을 나타낼 수 있다.
복수형은 용기나 단위를 나타내는 말을 복수로 만든다.

Paul and I want **a cup of tea** and **two glasses of milk**. Paul과 나는 / 차 한 잔과 / 우유 두 잔을 / 원한다.

Dad needed **two pieces of paper**.
아빠는 / 종이 두 장이 / 필요하셨다.

The children ate **five slices of cheese**.
그 어린이들은 / 치즈 다섯 조각을 / 먹었다.

Christopher and Susie ordered **three loaves of bread**. Christopher와 Susie는 / 빵 세 덩어리를 / 주문했다.

I bought **a pair of gloves** and **two pairs of pants**.
나는 / 장갑 한 켤레와 / 바지 두 벌을 / 샀다.

용기/단위	셀 수 없는 명사
a cup of	coffee, tea
a glass of	water, juice, milk, beer
a bottle of	water, juice, milk, wine, perfume
a piece of	pizza, cheese, cake, paper, advice, furniture, information, news
a slice of	pizza, cake, cheese, meat, bread
a loaf of	bread
a bowl of	salad, soup, rice
a bar of	soap, chocolate
a pair of	glasses, socks, shoes, gloves, jeans, pants

GRAMMAR CHECK

둘 중에서 어법에 맞는 것을 고르시오.

1. 저에게 커피 두 잔을 주세요.
   Please give me (two cup of coffees / two cups of coffee).
2. 나는 샐러드 두 그릇을 만들었다.
   I made (two bowls of salad / two bowls of salads).
3. 그는 매일 맥주 세 잔을 마신다.
   He drinks (three glass of beer / three glasses of beer) every day.
4. 그녀는 물 두 병을 샀다.
   She bought (two bottles of water / two bottles of waters).
5. 엄마는 양말 네 켤레가 필요하셨다.
   Mom needed (four pair of socks / four pairs of socks).
6. 그들은 가구 네 점을 옮겼다.
   They moved (four pieces of furniture / four pieces of furnitures).
7. 우리는 종이 세장을 원했다.
   We wanted (three pieces of paper / three piece of papers).
8. Jina는 빵 두 덩어리를 주문했다.
   Jina ordered (two loaves of bread / two loaves of breads).

01 주어진 단어를 사용하여 우리말에 맞게 문장을 완성하시오.

1. Jeffrey는 안경 하나를 구입했다. (pair, glasses)
   Jeffrey bought ______________________________ .

2. 나는 차 한잔을 즐겼다. (cup, tea)
   I enjoyed ______________________________ .

3. 남동생은 케이크 두 조각을 샀다. (piece, cake)
   My brother bought ______________________________ .

4. Pitt는 수프 두 그릇을 먹었다. (bowl, soup)
   Pitt ate ______________________________ .

5. 엄마는 빵 세 덩어리를 구우셨다. (loaf, bread)
   Mom baked ______________________________ .

6. 우리는 주스 네 잔을 주문했다. (glass, juice)
   We ordered ______________________________ .

7. 그 남자는 정보 하나를 들었다. (piece, information)
   The man heard ______________________________ .

02 틀린 부분을 바르게 고쳐 문장을 다시 쓰시오.

1. Lena made ten cup of coffee.
   ____

2. My sister exchanged six pair of jeans.
   ____

3. Julia received two bottle of perfumes.
   ____

4. They bought five slices of pizzas.
   ____

5. I gave four bars of soaps to Alicia.
   ____

6. The boy ate three bowls of rices.
   ____

03 우리말에 맞게 아래 글을 완성하시오.

Susie의 가족은 쇼핑센터에 갔다.
(1) 아빠는 청바지 한 벌을 사셨다.
(2) 엄마는 가구 세 점을 사셨다.
(3) Susie는 샐러드 두 그릇을 먹었다.
(4) Susie의 남동생은 비누 다섯 개를 샀다.

Susie's family went to the shopping center.

(1) ____________________

(2) ____________________

(3) ____________________

(4) ____________________

통합 서술형

● Paul과 Minsu가 먹은 메뉴를 보고 아래 글을 완성하시오.

Paul	pizza	juice	cake
Minsu	bread	water	soup

1. Paul ordered two pieces of pizza.
   He drank ____________________.
   He enjoyed ____________________.
2. Minsu ate ____________________.
   He drank ____________________.
   He had ____________________.

CORE 11 지시대명사 / 비인칭 주어 it

① it은 앞에 언급된 명사를 가리킬 때 쓴다.

There is a pen on the desk. **It** is mine. 책상 위에 / 펜이 / 있다. 그것은 / 내 것이다.

② this/these는 가까이에 있는 사람·사물을 가리킬 때, that/those는 멀리 있는 사람·사물을 가리킬 때 쓴다.

This is my sister, and **that** is your brother.
이 사람은 / 나의 여동생이고, 저 사람은 / 너의 남동생이다.

These are my shirts, and **those** are your hats.
이것들은 / 나의 셔츠들이고, 저것들은 / 너의 모자들이다.

it	그것
this/these	이것, 이 사람 / 이것들, 이 사람들
that/those	저것, 저 사람 / 저것들, 저 사람들

③ 비인칭 주어 it은 날씨, 시간, 요일, 온도, 날짜, 거리, 계절 등을 나타내는 문장의 주어로 쓰인다. '그것'으로 해석하지 않는다.

It is winter, but **it** is warm. 겨울이지만, 날이 / 따뜻하다.

GRAMMAR CHECK

주어진 단어를 사용하여 우리말에 맞게 문장을 완성하시오.

those　that　it　these　this

1. 엄마는 / 나에게 / 모자를 / 사주셨다. 나는 / 그것이 / 마음에 든다.
   Mom bought me a cap. I like ________________ .
2. 이것은 / 너의 과학책이니?
   Is ________________ your science book?
3. 저것은 / 너의 남동생의 노트북이니?
   Is ________________ your brother's laptop?
4. 이분들은 / Jenny의 조부모님들이다.
   ________________ are Jenny's grandparents.
5. 오늘은 / 12월 28일이다.
   ________________ is December 28th today.
6. 저것들은 / 피카소의 그림들이다.
   ________________ are Picasso's paintings.

01 밑줄 친 부분을 바르게 고쳐 문장을 다시 쓰시오.

1. I have a doll. That is pretty.

____

2. Are that your classmates?

____

3. That snows a lot in winter.

____

4. This leather shoes are very expensive.

____

5. Is these James' sister in the picture?

____

6. This is 2 kilometers from the station to the hospital.

____

02 주어진 단어를 사용하여 우리말에 맞게 문장을 완성하시오.

1. 지금 오스트레일리아는 봄이다. (spring)

   _______________ in Australia now.

2. 이분들은 나의 중학교 선생님들이다. (my teachers)

   _______________ from middle school.

3. Peter는 자전거가 한 대 있는데, 그것은 파란색이다. (blue)

   Peter has a bicycle and _______________ .

4. 집 밖은 춥고 바람이 부니? (cold and windy)

   _______________ outside the house?

5. 학교에서 버스 정류장까지 3킬로미터이다. (kilometers)

   _______________ from the school to the bus stop.

6. 이것들은 나의 연필들이고 저것들은 너의 펜들이다. (my pencils, your pens)

   _______________ and _______________ .

03 주어진 단어를 사용하여 우리말에 맞게 아래 일기를 완성하시오.

오늘은 일요일이었다.
밖은 따뜻하고 화창했다.
나는 Jason과 산책을 하다가 어떤 사람들과 마주쳤다.
Jason은 "이분은 나의 이모야."라고 말했다.
그리고 그는 "저 사람들은 나의 사촌들이야."라고 말했다.

____________________ today. (Sunday)

____________________ outside. (warm, sunny)

I took a walk with Jason and we saw some people.

Jason said, "____________________." (aunt)

And he said, "____________________." (cousin)

통합 서술형

그림을 보고 아래 대화를 완성하시오.

Mina: What is today's date?

Jinsu: ____________________

Mina: What time is it now?

Jinsu: ____________________

Mina: What is ____________________ on the table?

Jinsu: It is a vase.

Mina: What are ____________________ on the sofa?

Jinsu: They are robots.

CORE 12 재귀대명사

재귀대명사는 인칭대명사의 소유격이나 목적격에 -self/-selves를 붙인 형태로, '~자신', '직접'이라는 뜻이다.

	1인칭	2인칭	3인칭
단수	myself	yourself	himself / herself / itself
복수	ourselves	yourselves	themselves

① 재귀 용법: 주어와 목적어가 같을 때 목적어 자리에 쓴다.

She introduced **herself**. <동사의 목적어> 그녀는 / 그녀 자신을 / 소개했다.

I can take care of **myself**. <전치사의 목적어> 나는 / 나 자신을 / 돌볼 수 있다.

② 강조 용법: 주어, 목적어, 보어를 강조하기 위해 주어 다음이나 문장 끝에 쓰며, 생략이 가능하다.

He **himself** made the plans. 그가 / 직접 / 그 계획들을 / 만들었다.

GRAMMAR CHECK

우리말에 맞게 빈칸에 알맞은 재귀대명사를 쓰시오.

1. 나는 / 사진에서 / 나 자신을 / 보았다.
   I saw ____________ in the picture.
2. 그 남자가 / 직접 / 그 프로젝트를 / 끝냈다.
   The man ____________ finished the project.
3. Helen은 / 그녀 자신을 / 자랑스러워한다.
   Helen is proud of ____________.
4. 그들은 / 직접 / 그 기계를 / 만들었다.
   They made the machine ____________.
5. 너는 / 너 자신을 / 신뢰해야 한다.
   You should believe in ____________.

주요 관용 표현

by oneself 혼자, 스스로
of oneself 저절로
help oneself to 마음껏 먹다
for oneself 혼자 힘으로
enjoy oneself 즐기다
say to oneself 혼잣말하다

Check 알맞은 관용 표현을 쓰시오.

1. 혼자 힘으로 → ____________
2. 저절로 → ____________
3. 즐기다 → ____________

01 밑줄 친 부분을 바르게 고쳐 문장을 다시 쓰시오.

1. I me made the travel plans.

   ____

2. The window closed of it.

   ____

3. They enjoyed theirselves in the pool.

   ____

4. Did he finish the essay him?

   ____

5. The woman lives by her in the city.

   ____

6. My father and I painted the wall ourself.

   ____

02 재귀대명사와 주어진 단어를 사용하여 우리말에 맞게 문장을 완성하시오.

1. 그들은 그들 자신을 보호해야 한다. (protect)

   They should ______________________________ .

2. 나는 나 자신에게 편지를 썼다. (to, a letter)

   I wrote ______________________________ .

3. 이 사과들을 마음껏 드세요. (help)

   ______________________________ these apples.

4. 너는 혼자서 그 서점을 찾을 수 있니? (the bookstore)

   Can you find ______________________________ ?

5. 그들은 직접 그 상자들을 옮겼다. (moved, the boxes)

   They ______________________________ .

6. Timothy는 직접 부츠 한 켤레를 팔았다. (sold, pair, boots)

   Timothy ______________________________ .

03 주어진 단어를 사용하여 우리말에 맞게 문장을 쓰시오.

1. 

문이 저절로 열렸다. (open)

____

2. 

사람들은 공원에서 즐긴다. (at the park)

____

3. 

그는 혼자 달린다. (run)

____

4. 

쿠키들을 마음껏 드세요. (cookies)

____

통합 서술형

Risa의 일기를 읽고 틀린 곳을 4군데 찾아 문장을 바르게 고쳐 쓰시오.

Mom invited my grandparents to our house last Saturday.
Mom and I cooked chicken and salad myself.
My brother made lemonade of himself.
My grandparents helped them in the dishes.
We enjoyed usselves at dinner.

1. ______________________________
2. ______________________________
3. ______________________________
4. ______________________________

CORE 13 부정대명사

1. one: 앞에 나온 셀 수 있는 명사를 대신한다. 복수형은 ones이다.

I need a pen. Can I have **one**? – How about **ones** over there?
나는 / 펜이 / 필요해. 하나 / 가질 수 있을까? — 저기에 있는 것들은 / 어때?

2. another: 같은 종류의 또 다른 것(하나 더)를 의미한다.

This skirt is too short. Can you show me **another**? 이 치마는 / 너무 / 짧아요. 제게 / 또 다른 것을 / 보여주시겠어요?

3. the other(s) / others: the other는 나머지 하나, the others는 나머지 전부, others는 다른 사람(것)들을 의미한다.

I just need one. You can take **the others**. 나는 / 하나만 / 필요해. 나머지 전부는 / 네가 / 가져도 돼.

GRAMMAR CHECK

부정대명사를 사용하여 우리말에 맞게 문장을 완성하시오.

one others the others another

1. Paul은 / 그의 지갑을 / 잃어버렸다. 그는 / 하나를 / 사야 한다.
   Paul lost his wallet. He has to buy ____________ .
2. 이 오렌지는 / 맛이 좋네요. 하나 더 / 먹을 수 있을까요?
   This orange tastes good. Can I have ____________ ?
3. 그 남자는 / 다른 사람들을 / 돕는 것을 / 좋아한다.
   The man likes helping ____________ .
4. 바나나가 / 네 개 있다. 하나는 / 신선하지만, 나머지 전부는 / 그렇지 않다.
   There are four bananas. One is fresh, and ____________ are not.

주요 관용 표현

one ~, the other ...	하나는 ~, 나머지 하나는 …
one ~, the others ...	하나는 ~, 나머지 전부는 …
one ~, another ..., the other _	(셋 중) 하나는 ~, 또 다른 하나는 …, 나머지 하나는 _
some ~, others ...	일부는 ~, 또 다른 일부는 …
some ~, the others ...	일부는 ~, 나머지 전부는 …

Check 둘 중 어법에 맞는 것을 고르시오.

1. I have two friends. (One / Some) is Clara, (the other / other) is Tommy.
2. (One / Some) drank tea, others drank coffee.

01 우리말에 맞게 빈칸에 알맞은 부정대명사를 쓰시오.

1. 이 블라우스는 너무 끼어요. 또 다른 것을 볼 수 있을까요?
   This blouse is too tight. Can I see ______________ ?

2. 쿠키 다섯 개가 있었다. 내가 두 개를 먹었고, 남동생이 나머지 전부를 먹었다.
   There were five cookies. I ate two, and my brother ate ______________ .

3. Nana는 네 명의 친구가 있다. 한 명은 의사이고, 나머지 전부는 교사들이다.
   Nana has four friends. ______________ is a doctor, and ______________ are teachers.

4. 일부는 봄을 좋아하고, 또 다른 일부는 가을을 좋아한다.
   ______________ love spring, and ______________ love fall.

5. 나는 드레스 세 벌이 있다. 하나는 빨강이고, 또 다른 하나는 노랑이고, 나머지 하나는 검정이다.
   I have three dresses. ______________ is red, ______________ is yellow, and ______________ is black.

6. 이 가방들은 너무 무거워요. 가벼운 것들을 보여주시겠어요?
   These bags are too heavy. Can you show me light ______________ ?

02 틀린 부분을 바르게 고쳐 문장을 다시 쓰시오.

1. This ring is big. Do you have a smaller another?
   ____

2. I have two balls. One is blue, and other is red.
   ____

3. We should try to be helpful to another.
   ____

4. Some like mountains, and other like rivers.
   ____

5. The shoes are large. I'll try smaller one.
   ____

6. She has three presents. One is for Bob, another is for Jin, and other is for Tim.
   ____

03 다음 우리말에 맞게 문장을 쓰시오.

1. 하나는 책이고, 나머지 하나는 앨범이다.

____

2. 일부는 음악을 좋아하고, 나머지 전부는 미술을 좋아한다.

____

3. 하나는 의자이고, 또 다른 하나는 책상이고, 나머지 하나는 탁자이다.

____

4. 일부는 커피를 마셨고, 또 다른 일부는 차를 마셨다.

____

5. 하나는 자동차이고, 나머지 전부는 버스들이다.

____

통합 서술형

주어진 단어를 사용하여 그림을 설명하는 글을 완성하시오.

1. 

2. 

3. 

1. Jina has friends.
   One is a girl, and ______________________________.
2. There are three fruit on the table.
   ____
3. Tim has two pets.
   ____

one	the others	another	the other

CORE 14 형용사와 부사

Chapter 05

형용사와 부사

CORE 15 수량 형용사

CORE 14 형용사와 부사

1 형용사는 명사 앞이나 뒤에서 명사를 수식하거나 설명한다.

Kevin is a **diligent** student. <명사 수식>
Kevin은 / 성실한 / 학생이다.

I want something **cold**. <명사 수식>
나는 / 차가운 / 것을 / 원한다.

The zookeeper is **happy** with the animals. <설명-주격보어>
그 사육사는 / 동물들과 함께 / 행복하다.

한정적 용법	· 보통은 명사 앞에서 수식한다. · -thing, -one, -body로 끝나는 대명사는 뒤에서 수식한다.
서술적 용법	· 주격보어나 목적격보어로 쓰여 명사를 보충 설명한다.

2 부사는 형용사, 다른 부사, 동사 또는 문장 전체를 수식한다.

He is **seriously** ill. <형용사 수식> 그는 / 매우 / 아프다.

I **often** walk to school. <동사 수식>
나는 / 종종 / 학교에 / 걸어간다.

Luckily, I arrived in time. <문장 전체 수식>
다행히도 / 나는 / 시간 맞춰 / 도착했다.

형용사와 형태가 같은 부사		
high 높은/높게 *cf.* highly 매우	hard 열심인/열심히 hardly 거의 ~않다	near 가까운/가까이 nearly 거의

빈도부사(일의 발생 정도를 나타내는 부사)

always > usually > often > sometimes > hardly > never
(항상) (대개) (종종) (가끔) (거의 ~않다) (절대 ~않다)

· be동사/조동사 뒤, 일반동사 앞에 온다.

GRAMMAR CHECK

주어진 단어를 바르게 배열하여 우리말에 맞게 문장을 완성하시오.

1. 그 새는 / 가슴에 / 화려한 / 털이 / 있다. (the bird, feathers, has, colorful)
 ______________________ on its chest.
2. 그 책은 / 나에게 / 흥미로워 / 보인다. (seems, interesting, the book)
 ______________________ to me.
3. 그는 / 어제 / 유명한 / 사람을 / 봤다. (he, famous, someone, saw)
 ______________________ yesterday.
4. 그녀는 / 항상 / 도서관에서 / 공부한다. (studies, she, always)
 ______________________ at the library.

형용사를 부사로 만드는 방법

대부분의 형용사	+ -ly	most – most**ly**
「자음+y」로 끝나는 형용사	y → i + -ly	easy – easi**ly**
-le로 끝나는 형용사	-le → -ly	gentle – gent**ly**

Check 주어진 형용사를 부사로 바꾸어 쓰시오.

1. beautiful → ____________
2. heavy → ____________
3. comfortable → ____________

01

밑줄 친 부분을 바르게 고쳐 문장을 다시 쓰시오.

1. Your voice sounds strangely to me.

   ____

2. She can't eat cold anything.

   ____

3. The student is late often for school.

   ____

4. The young students are really smartly.

   ____

5. Surprising, he passed the exam.

   ____

6. William never will know the secret.

   ____

02

주어진 단어를 사용하여 우리말에 맞게 문장을 완성하시오

1. Sharon은 나를 기쁘게 맞이한다. (greet, happy)

   Sharon ______________________________ .

2. 그 야구 선수는 열심히 연습한다. (practice, hard)

   The baseball player ______________________________ .

3. 그 콘서트는 거의 끝났다. (be, near)

   The concert ______________________________ over.

4. 이 블라우스는 내 치마와 완벽하게 어울린다. (match, perfect)

   ______________________________ with my skirt.

5. 그는 요즘 자신의 차를 거의 운전하지 않는다. (drive, hard)

   ______________________________ his car these days.

6. 나는 내일 늦게까지 일할 것이다. (work, late)

   ______________________________ tomorrow.

03 주어진 단어를 사용하여 우리말에 맞게 아래 글을 완성하시오.

나에게는 멋진 가족이 있다.
아빠는 성실한 정비공이다. 그는 자신의 일터에서 항상 열심히 일한다.
엄마는 훌륭한 요리사이다. 그녀는 맛있는 것을 만들어낸다.
내 남동생은 놀랍도록 지저분하다. 그는 자신의 방을 거의 치우지 않는다.
하지만 나는 부모님을 사랑하는 것처럼 남동생도 사랑한다.

I have a wonderful family.
Dad is a hard-working mechanic.
He always ______________________ at his workplace. (hard)
Mom ______________________. (chef, great)
She ______________________. (delicious, something)
My brother ______________________. (messy, surprising)
He ______________________ his room. (hard, clean)
But I love my brother just like I love my parents.

통합 서술형

Ben의 방학 중 여가활동표를 보고 주어진 단어를 한 번씩만 사용하여 문장을 완성하시오.

	MON	TUE	WED	THU	FRI	SAT	SUN
play the piano	√	√	√	√	√	√	√
read books		√	√	√	√	√	√
ride a bike	√			√		√	√
volunteer at the library		√			√		
play computer games							

1. Ben ______________________ the piano.
2. He ______________________ books.
3. He ______________________ his bike.
4. He ______________________ at the library.
5. He ______________________ computer games.

always usually often sometimes never

CORE 15 수량 형용사

● 명사 앞에 쓰여 그 수와 양을 나타내는 형용사를 수량 형용사라고 한다. 명사의 종류에 따라 앞에 올 수 있는 수량 형용사가 다르다.

We prepared **many** potatoes and **much** butter.
우리는 / 많은 / 감자와 / 많은 / 버터를 / 준비했다.

The teacher brought **a few** cups and **a little** water.
그 교사는 / 조금의 / 컵과 / 조금의 / 물을 / 가져왔다.

The district has **few** trees and **little** water.
그 지역은 / 나무도 / 거의 없고 / 물도 / 거의 없다.

She has **some** cookies.
그녀는 / 약간의 / 과자가 / 있다.

I don't have **any** milk, but would you like **some** tea?
나는 / 약간의 / 우유도 / 가지고 있지 / 않은데, / 차를 / 좀 / 마시겠어요?

수	many / a few / few + 셀 수 있는 명사 (많은) (조금 있는) (거의 없는)
양	much / a little / little + 셀 수 없는 명사 (많은) (조금 있는) (거의 없는)
수·양	a lot of(lots of) + 셀 수 있는/없는 명사 (많은)

긍정문, 권유의 의문문	some(약간의) + 셀 수 있는/없는 명사
부정문, 의문문	any(약간의) + 셀 수 있는/없는 명사

GRAMMAR CHECK ● **주어진 수량 형용사를 한 번씩만 써서 우리말에 맞게 문장을 완성하시오.**

much / many / a little / a few / little / few / any

1. Anna는 / 많은 / 나라들을 / 여행했다.
   Anna traveled through ________________ countries.
2. 몇몇 / 학생들이 / 그 강연에 / 참석했다.
   ________________ students attended the lecture.
3. Sam은 / 도서관에서 / 책을 / 거의 빌리지 않았다.
   Sam borrowed ________________ books from the library.
4. 그 남자는 / 자선 단체에 / 조금의 / 돈을 / 기부했다.
   The man donated ________________ money to a charity.
5. 그는 / 연습 후에 / 많은 / 물을 / 마신다.
   He drinks ________________ water after practice.
6. 작년 겨울에 / 눈이 / 거의 오지 않았다.
   We had ________________ snow last winter.
7. 그녀는 / 약간의 / 정보도 / 얻지 못했다.
   She did not get ________________ information.

01

둘 중에서 어법에 맞는 것을 고르시오.

1. They gave (some / any) clothes to the poor children.
2. He didn't spend (some / any) time in the pool.
3. Mark solved (many / much) problems in 10 minutes.
4. Olivia said (a few / a little) things about her school days.
5. We've had (many / much) rain this summer.
6. I put (a few / a little) flour in the bowl.
7. (Few / Little) people heard the sound.
8. She didn't put (many / much) dressing on the salad.
9. Did you get (some / any) advice about the project?
10. There is (few / little) food in the refrigerator.

02

틀린 부분을 바르게 고쳐 문장을 다시 쓰시오.

1. Much foreigners visited the place today.

   ____

2. Janet didn't buy some bread at the bakery.

   ____

3. He put a few salt into the soup.

   ____

4. The child spilled many juice on the table.

   ____

5. The painter sold little paintings in his lifetime.

   ____

6. I have no fruit, but she has any bananas.

   ____

03 다음 우리말에 맞게 문장을 쓰시오.

오늘 친구들과 나는 함께 점심을 먹었다.
Paul은 많은 핫도그를 먹었다.
(1) Jane은 핫도그를 조금 먹었다.
(2) 나는 핫도그를 거의 먹지 않았다.
(3) Paul은 약간의 우유를 마셨다.
(4) Jane은 우유를 거의 마시지 않았다.
(5) 나는 많은 우유를 마셨다.

Today my friends and I had lunch together.
Paul ate many hot dogs.
(1) ______________________________
(2) ______________________________
(3) ______________________________
(4) ______________________________
(5) ______________________________

통합 서술형

그림을 보고 주어진 단어를 한 번씩만 사용하여 문장을 완성하시오.

1. Sara bought ______________ bread.
2. But Jack only bought ______________ .
   She also bought vegetables.
3. She made ______________ sandwiches.
4. But he didn't make ______________ .
5. She said to him, "Would you like ______________ sandwiches?"

much　a few　a little　some　any　bread　sandwiches

Chapter
06
비교

CORE 16 형용사·부사의 비교급과 최상급

CORE 17 비교급·최상급의 주요 표현

CORE 18 원급의 주요 표현

CORE 16 형용사·부사의 비교급과 최상급

비교급(더 ~한/하게)은 형용사·부사에 -er을 붙이고, 최상급(가장 ~한)은 -est를 붙여 만든다. 비교급 뒤에는 than이 오고, 최상급 앞에는 the가 온다.

He is **tall**. <원급>
그는 / 키가 크다.

He is **taller** than Jack. <비교급>
그는 / Jack보다 / 더 키가 크다.

He is the **tallest** in the class. <최상급>
그는 / 학급에서 / 가장 키가 크다.

	비교급	최상급
대부분의 형용사·부사	+ -er	+ -est
-e로 끝나면	+ -r	+ -st
「단모음+단자음」으로 끝나면	+ 단자음 + -er	+ 단자음 + -est
-y로 끝나면	y → i + -er	y → i + -est
2음절 대부분 / 3음절 이상	more + 원급	most + 원급
「형용사 + -ly」의 부사	more + 원급	most + 원급

GRAMMAR CHECK 주어진 단어를 사용하여 우리말에 맞게 빈칸에 알맞은 말을 쓰시오

1. 내 고양이는 / 네 고양이보다 / 더 작다. (small)
   My cat is ______________ than your cat.
2. 오늘이 / 지난 10년 중 / 가장 추운 / 날이다. (cold)
   Today is the ______________ day in ten years.
3. 여기서는 / 야구가 / 축구보다 / 더 인기 있다. (popular)
   Baseball is ______________ ______________ than soccer here.
4. 내 남동생의 방은 / 내 방보다 / 더 더럽다. (dirty)
   My brother's room is ______________ than mine.
5. 그녀는 / 가장 자신 있게 / 질문에 대답했다. (confidently)
   She answered the question the ______________ ______________.

불규칙 변화하는 형용사와 부사

- good/well – better – best
  좋은/좋게 더 좋은/좋게 최고의/최고로
- little – less – least
  적은 더 적은 최소의
- late 늦은
  - later – latest (시간) 나중의 최신의
  - latter – last (순서) 후자의 마지막의
- bad/badly – worse – worst
  나쁜/나쁘게 더 나쁜/나쁘게 최악의/최악으로
- many/much – more – most
  많은 더 많은 가장 많은
- far 먼
  - farther – farthest (거리) 더 먼 가장 먼
  - further – furthest (정도) 더 이상의 최대한의

Check 비교급과 최상급을 쓰시오.

1. good – __________ – __________
2. little – __________ – __________
3. much – __________ – __________
4. badly – __________ – __________
5. late (시간) – __________ – __________

01

주어진 단어를 사용하여 우리말에 맞게 문장을 완성하시오.

1. 너의 방은 나의 방보다 더 따뜻하다. (warm)
   Your room is ______________________ my room.

2. 이 하얀색 강아지가 세 마리 중 가장 귀엽다. (cute)
   This white puppy is ______________________ of the three.

3. 오월은 나에게 일 년 중 가장 바쁜 달이다. (busy)
   May is ______________________ month of the year for me.

4. 빨간 공이 그 공들 중에서 가장 크다. (big)
   The red ball is ______________________ of the balls.

5. 네 노트북이 내 것보다 더 좋다. (good)
   Your laptop is ______________________ mine.

6. 최신 소식은 무엇인가요? (late)
   What is ______________________ news?

7. 내 생각엔 언어적 폭력은 신체적 폭력보다 더 나쁘다. (bad)
   I think verbal violence is ______________________ physical violence.

02

틀린 부분을 바르게 고쳐 문장을 다시 쓰시오.

1. She is young than my sister.
   ____

2. Her idea is most creative in our company.
   ____

3. This bed is the comfortablest.
   ____

4. Jane fixed the problem carefully than you.
   ____

5. David's book is most interesting than that book.
   ____

6. Walter is the most old player on the team.
   ____

03 표를 보고 주어진 단어를 사용하여 <보기>와 같이 문장을 완성하시오.

	Price	Width
Table A	$110	70cm
Table B	$90	90cm
Table C	$130	80cm

보기 Table A is cheaper than Table C. (cheap)

Table B is the widest of the three. (wide)

1. Table A is ____________ Table B. (expensive)

   Table A is ____________ of the three. (narrow)

2. Table B is ____________ of the three. (cheap)

3. Table C is ____________ Table A. (wide)

   Table C is ____________ of the three. (expensive)

통합 서술형

● 다음 세 마리 개의 몸집과 나이를 참조하여 아래 글을 완성하시오.

<Max - 6>

<Vino - 6>

<Bota - 10>

1. Max is big. Max ____________ Vino and Bota.

   Max ____________ of the three.

   Vino is small. Vino ____________ Bota.

   Vino ____________ of the three.

2. Vino and Max are 6 years old.

   They ____________ Bota.

   Bota ____________ of the three.

CORE 17 비교급·최상급의 주요 표현

① 비교급을 이용한 주요 표현

Math is less difficult than history for me.
나에게는 / 수학이 / 역사보다 / 덜 어렵다.

The older you grow, the wiser you become.
더 나이가 들수록 / 더 현명해진다.

She drove her car faster and faster. 그녀는 / 점점 더 빠르게 / 차를 몰았다.

less+형용사·부사+than	…보다 덜 ~한(하게)
the+비교급, the+비교급	더 ~할수록 더 …한(하게)
비교급+and+비교급	점점 더 ~한(하게)

② 최상급을 이용한 주요 표현

Jack is the least diligent of the students.
Jack은 / 학생들 중에서 / 가장 덜 성실하다.

Plastic is one of the most useful inventions.
플라스틱은 / 가장 유용한 발명품들 중 / 하나이다.

The Nile is the second longest river in the world. 나일강은 / 세상에서 / 두 번째로 가장 긴 강이다.

the least+형용사·부사	가장 덜 ~한(하게)
one of the+최상급+복수 명사	가장 ~한 …중 하나
the+서수+최상급	…번 째로 가장 ~한

GRAMMAR CHECK

주어진 단어를 바르게 배열하여 우리말에 맞게 문장을 완성하시오.

1. Bobby는 / 그의 형보다 / 덜 인기 있다. (his brother, less, than, popular)
   Bobby is ______________________________.
2. 그는 / 인부들 중에서 / 가장 덜 게으르다. (is, lazy, the least)
   He ______________________________ of the workers.
3. 더 많이 먹을수록 / 더 뚱뚱해진다. (the, the, fatter, more)
   ______________ you eat, ______________ you become.
4. 우리는 / 그곳에서 / 가장 안전한 장소들 중 / 하나를 / 찾았다. (the safest, of, places, one)
   We found ______________________________ there.
5. 그 밧줄이 / 점점 더 가늘어진다. (thinner, getting, and, thinner)
   The rope is ______________________________.
6. Adam은 / 도서관에서 / 다섯 번째로 두꺼운 책을 / 읽었다. (book, thickest, the fifth)
   Adam read ______________________________ in the library.

01

밑줄 친 부분을 바르게 고쳐 문장을 다시 쓰시오.

1. His health is getting good and good.

   ____

2. It is less warmest today than yesterday.

   ____

3. He has the fourth strong arm of the students.

   ____

4. Saturn is one of the largest planet in the solar system.

   ____

5. The high we went up, the cold we felt.

   ____

6. The moment was the least happiest of my life.

   ____

02

주어진 단어를 사용하여 우리말에 맞게 문장을 완성하시오.

1. 천연가스는 석탄보다 덜 저렴하다. (cheap)
   Natural gas is ____________________ coal.

2. 날씨가 점점 더 더워진다. (hot)
   The weather is getting ____________________.

3. 고비 사막은 지구상에서 가장 큰 사막들 중 하나이다. (large, desert)
   The Gobi is ____________________ on earth.

4. 그 시는 그녀의 시집 안에서 가장 덜 어렵다. (difficult)
   The poem is ____________________ in her collection of poetry.

5. Susan은 학생들 중에서 세 번째로 총명하다. (intelligent)
   Susan ____________________ among the students.

6. 그 책이 더 오래될수록 가치는 더 높아진다. (old, high)
   __________ the book is, __________ the value is.

03 주어진 단어를 사용하여 우리말에 맞게 문장을 완성하시오.

우리 학교 농구부 선수인 Kevin을 소개할게요.
그는 팀에서 두 번째로 어려요.
그는 선수들 중에서 가장 덜 게을러요.
그는 더 많이 연습할수록 더 높게 점프해요.
그리고 그는 점점 더 빨라지고 있어요. (get, fast)
그는 팀에서 가장 잘하는 선수들 중 한 명이에요.

Let me introduce our school basketball player Kevin.

He is ____________________ on the team.

He is the least lazy of the players.

__________ he practices, ____________________.

And ____________________.

____

통합 서술형

● 표를 보고 주어진 단어를 사용하여 아래 글을 완성하시오.

	Andy	Tina	Joel	Becky
Height	170cm	165cm	160cm	155cm
Weight	55kg	60kg	50kg	45kg

1. Andy is the tallest of all. (tall)

   Tina is __________ tall __________ Andy.

   Joel is the third __________ of all.

   Becky is ____________________ of all.

2. Tina is the heaviest of all. (heavy)

   Joel is ____________________ Tina.

   Andy is ____________________ of all.

   Becky is ____________________ of all.

CORE 18 원급의 주요 표현

Sammy is as strong as I (am).
Sammy는 / 나만큼 / 힘이 세다.

A stream is not as(so) deep as a river.
개울은 / 강만큼 / 깊지 않다.

I jumped as high as possible.
(= as high as I could)
나는 / 가능한 한 높게 / 점프했다.

as+원급+as	…만큼 ~한(하게)
not as(so)+원급+as	…만큼 ~하지 않는(않게)
as+원급+as possible = as+원급+as+주어+can	가능한 한 ~하게

GRAMMAR CHECK

주어진 단어를 바르게 배열하여 우리말에 맞게 문장을 완성하시오.

1. 중국어는 / 영어만큼 / 어렵다. (difficult, as, English, as)
   Chinese is ______________________ .

2. Patricia는 / 자신의 언니만큼 / 영리하지 않다. (as, not, as, smart, her sister)
   Patricia is ______________________ .

3. 나는 / 가능한 한 조용히 / 걸었다. (as, I could, as, quietly)
   I walked ______________________ .

4. James는 / 나만큼 / 빨리 / 헤엄친다. (as, me, as, fast)
   James swims ______________________ .

5. 그 선생님은 / 가능한 한 천천히 / 말했다. (possible, as, as, slowly)
   The teacher spoke ______________________ .

6. 아빠는 / 일주일 전만큼 / 바쁘지 않다. (busy, not, so, as, a week ago)
   Dad is ______________________ .

7. 그는 / 가능한 한 많이 / 연습한다. (much, as, he, as, can)
   He practices ______________________ .

8. 그녀는 / 나만큼 / 주의 깊게 / 경청했다. (carefully, I, as, did, as)
   She listended ______________________ .

01 주어진 단어를 사용하여 우리말에 맞게 문장을 완성하시오.

1. 그 울타리는 그 건물만큼 높다. (tall)
   The fence is ______________________ the building.
2. 이 음식은 저 것만큼 맵지 않다. (spicy)
   This dish is ______________________ that one.
3. 나는 요즘 가능한 한 일찍 일어난다. (early)
   I get up ______________________ these days.
4. 너의 목걸이는 내 것만큼 멋지다. (attractive)
   Your necklace is ______________________ mine.
5. Anna는 그 고객에게 가능한 한 예의 바르게 말했다. (politely)
   Anna talked ______________________ to the customer.
6. 할아버지는 할머니만큼 오래 사시지 못했다. (live, long)
   My grandfather did ______________________ my grandmother.

02 틀린 부분을 바르게 고쳐 문장을 다시 쓰시오.

1. Philosophy is as more important as science.
   ____
2. I will call you back as quickly than I can.
   ____
3. Sharks are as not big as whales.
   ____
4. These peaches are so sweet as honey.
   ____
5. She solved the problem as sooner as possible.
   ____
6. My sister does not work as actively so my brother.
   ____

03 우리말에 맞게 아래 일기를 완성하시오.

Saturday, July 17th

내 친구에게는 고양이 Barbie가 있다. 나에게는 고양이 Minky가 있다.
Minky는 매우 귀엽고 빠르다.
Barbie는 Minky만큼 귀엽다.
그러나 Barbie는 Minky만큼 빠르지 않다.
내 친구와 나는 그들을 굉장히 사랑한다.
그래서 우리는 가능한 한 많이 그들과 놀아준다.

My friend has his cat Barbie. I have my cat Minky.
Minky is very cute and fast.

____

But ____.

My friend and I love them very much.

So ____.

통합 서술형

● 주어진 단어를 사용하여 다음 두 탁자를 비교하는 글을 완성하시오.

Table A

< 60kg - $120 >

Table B

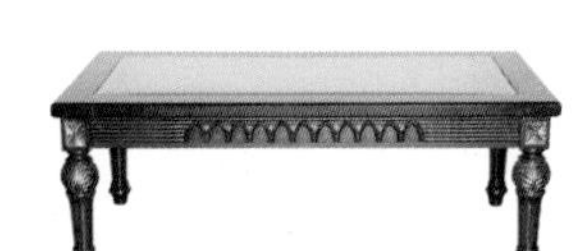

< 60kg - $120 >

1. Table A ______________________ Table B. (heavy)

   Table A ______________________ Table B. (wide)

2. Table B ______________________ Table A. (expensive)

   Table B ______________________ Table A. (high)

Chapter 07

문장의 종류

CORE 19 의문사가 있는 의문문

CORE 20 명령문 / 권유문 / 감탄문

CORE 21 부가의문문 / 선택의문문

CORE 19 의문사가 있는 의문문

● '누가, 무엇을, 언제, 어디서, 왜, 어떻게' 같은 정보를 물을 때는 의문사를 사용한다.

Who is she? – She is my teacher.
그녀는 / 누구니? – 나의 선생님이야.

What do you want? – I want milk.
무엇을 / 원하니? – 우유를 / 원해.

When is your birthday?
– It's on March 27th. 네 생일은 / 언제니? – 3월 27일이야.

Where do you live? – I live in Seoul. 너는 / 어디에 / 사니? – 서울에 / 살아.

Why are you sad? – My mom is sick. 너는 / 왜 / 우울하니? – 엄마가 / 아프셔.

How do you go to school? – I go to school on foot. 너는 / 어떻게 / 학교에 / 가니? – 나는 / 걸어서 / 학교에 / 가.

종류	who	what	when	where	why	how
	누구	무엇	언제	어디서	왜	어떻게
어순	의문사+be동사+주어 ~?					
	의문사+do/does/did+주어+동사원형 ~?					

대답은 Yes/No로 하지 않고 그 의문사에 대응하는 내용이어야 한다.

GRAMMAR CHECK

● 우리말에 맞게 빈칸에 알맞은 의문사를 쓰시오.

1. 그 / 키 큰 소녀는 / 누구니? → __________ is the tall girl?
2. 그는 / 무엇을 / 가지고 있지? → __________ does he have?
3. 너는 / 어디 / 출신이니? → __________ are you from?
4. 네 수업은 / 언제 / 시작하니? → __________ does your class start?
5. 오늘 / 날씨는 / 어떠니? → __________ is the weather today?
6. 너는 / 왜 / 컴퓨터가 / 필요하니? → __________ do you need a computer?

「How + 형용사/부사」로 가격, 개수, 나이 등을 묻을 수 있다.

How	much	가격/양	**How much** is the cell phone? 그 휴대전화는 / 얼마인가요?
	many	개수	
	old	나이	**How old** are you? 너는 / 몇 살이니?
	tall	키	
	long	길이/기간	**How often** does the bus come? 버스는 / 얼마나 자주 / 오나요?
	far	거리	
	often	빈도	

Check 빈칸에 알맞은 말을 쓰시오.

1. How __________ is your brother?
   네 형은 몇 살이니?
2. How __________ is your school from your home? 네 학교는 집에서 얼마나 머니?
3. How __________ students are there?
   몇 명의 학생들이 있니?

01

우리말에 맞게 주어진 단어를 바르게 배열하시오.

1. 우체국은 어디에 있니? (is, where, the post office)

____

2. 저쪽에 있는 저 남자는 누구니? (the man, who, is, over there)

____

3. 그 뮤지컬은 언제 끝났니? (end, when, did, the musical)

____

4. 네가 가장 좋아하는 색깔은 무엇이니? (is, what, your, favorite color)

____

5. 사람들은 왜 그 코미디언을 싫어하나요? (hate, why, people, do, the comedian)

____

6. 그는 얼마나 자주 영화를 보러 가나요? (he, does, how often, go, to the movies)

____

02

의문사와 주어진 단어를 사용하여 우리말에 맞게 문장을 쓰시오.

1. 저 개는 몇 살이니? (the dog)

____

2. 그 음악회는 언제 시작하나요? (the concert, start)

____

3. 너의 할아버지는 어디에 사시니? (grandfather, live)

____

4. 그들은 점심으로 무엇을 먹었니? (eat for lunch)

____

5. 네가 가장 좋아하는 가수는 누구니? (singer)

____

6. 너는 얼마나 많은 나라를 방문했니? (countries, visit)

____

03 대화가 자연스럽게 이어지도록 틀린 부분을 바르게 고쳐 문장을 다시 쓰시오.

1. A: When are you from? → ____________________
   B: I'm from the USA.

2. A: How is her name? → ____________________
   B: Her name is Barbara.

3. A: How tall is your brother? → ____________________
   B: He is 15 years old.

4. A: What are you so happy? → ____________________
   B: Because I got an A on my test.

5. A: Where did you buy the bike? → ____________________
   B: I bought it last year.

통합 서술형

◎ **Maureen을 소개한 표를 보고 아래 대화를 완성하시오.**

이름	Maureen
국적	Canada
나이	14 years old
가족 수	5
여가 활동	play the violin

George : What is your name?
Maureen : My name is ____________.
George : ________ ________ ________ from?
Maureen : I am from ________.
George : ________ ________ ________ you ?
Maureen : I am 14 years old.
George : ________ ________ people are there in your family?
Maureen : There are five people.
George : ________ do you do in your free time?
Maureen : I ________ ________ ________.

CORE 20 명령문 / 권유문 / 감탄문

① 명령문: 상대방에게 지시, 명령할 때 쓰는 문장으로 주어인 You를 생략한다.

Be quiet. Don't talk in the library.
조용히 해라. 도서관에서는 / 말하지 / 마라.

Please come by 10 o'clock.
Never be late. 10시까지 / 오세요. 늦지 / 마세요.

긍정 명령문	동사원형 ~.	~해라.
부정 명령문	Don't(Never)+동사원형 ~.	~하지 말아라.
부드럽게 명령할 때나 부탁할 때는 명령문 앞이나 뒤에 please를 붙인다.		

② 권유문: 상대방에게 권유, 제안할 때 쓴다.

Let's hurry. Let's not waste time.
서두르자. 시간을 / 낭비하지 / 말자.

긍정 권유문	Let's+동사원형 ~.	~하자.
부정 권유문	Let's not+동사원형 ~.	~하지 말자.

③ 감탄문: '정말 ~하구나!'라는 뜻으로 놀람, 기쁨, 슬픔 등의 감정을 표현한다.

What a tall boy (he is)! (그는) 정말 / 키가 큰 / 소년이구나!
What pretty dolls you have!
너는 / 정말 / 예쁜 / 인형들을 / 가졌구나!

How exciting (the movie is)! (그 영화는) / 정말 / 재밌구나!
How fast she runs! 그녀는 / 정말 / 빨리 / 달리는구나!

what 감탄문	What (a/an)+형용사+명사(+주어+동사)! What+형용사+복수명사(+주어+동사)!
how 감탄문	How+형용사/부사(+주어+동사)!

GRAMMAR CHECK

다음 문장을 지시대로 바꾸어 쓰시오.

1. You clean your room. (명령문)

2. You walk on the grass. (부정 명령문)

3. We go for a swim. (권유문)

4. We don't close the windows. (권유문)

5. This cake is very delicious. (how 감탄문)

6. It is a very huge dog. (what 감탄문)

01 틀린 부분을 바르게 고쳐 문장을 다시 쓰시오.

1. Do kindly to your neighbors.

2. Let go hiking on Sunday.

3. Eat not junk food.

4. Not let's play computer games.

5. How an exciting story it is!

6. What beautifully Jasmine sings!

02 주어진 단어를 사용하여 우리말에 맞게 감탄문을 쓰시오.

1. 정말 멋진 선물이구나! (what, gift, nice)

2. 정말 똑똑한 학생들이구나! (what, students, smart)

3. 그 아기는 정말 귀엽구나! (how, cute)

4. 그 집들은 정말 아름답구나! (how, beautiful)

5. 너는 정말 커다란 우산을 가졌구나! (what, have, umbrella, big)

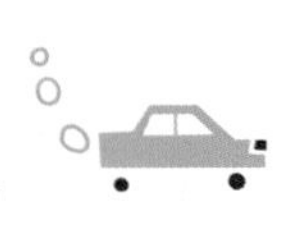

6. 그 차는 정말 빨리 달리는구나! (go, fast)

03 주어진 단어를 사용하여 우리말에 맞게 문장을 완성하시오.

1. 다시는 늦지 말아라. (late)

 ______________________________ again.

2. 방과 후에 농구를 하자. (basketball)

 ______________________________ after school.

3. 절대 그 문을 열지 말아라. (never)

 ______________________________ the door.

4. 도서관에서는 시끄럽게 말하지 말자. (talk loudly)

 ______________________________ in the library.

5. 저녁을 먹기 전에 손을 씻으세요. (please, wash)

 ______________________________ before dinner.

통합 서술형

주어진 단어를 사용하여 그림과 일치하도록 미술관 안내문을 완성하시오.

NOTICE

Welcome to Great Art Gallery.

__________ great paintings we have!

__________ wonderful they are!

Please keep quiet and follow the rules.

1. __________ your cell phone in the gallery.
2. __________ the paintings.
3. __________ pictures.

touch	how	what	turn off	take

CORE 21 부가의문문 / 선택의문문

① 부가의문문: 어떤 말 뒤에 '그렇지?' 또는 '그렇지 않니?'라는 의미로 상대방에게 확인하거나 동의를 구할 때 덧붙이는 말이다.

You are busy today, **aren't you?** 너는 / 오늘 / 바쁘지, 그렇지 / 않니?

He doesn't like this novel, **does he?**
그는 / 이 소설을 / 좋아하지 / 않지, 그렇지?

Pass me the salt, **will you?** 소금 좀 / 건네줘, 알았지?

Let's go on a picnic, **shall we?** 소풍 가자, 그럴 거지?

앞문장	부가의문문
긍정문	, 부정형 동사+주어?
부정문	, 동사+주어?
명령문	, will you?
Let's ~	, shall we?

- 동사: be동사와 조동사는 그대로 사용, 일반동사는 do동사 사용
- 부정형 동사: 반드시 축약형 사용
- 주어: 반드시 인칭대명사 사용

② 선택의문문: 둘 중 하나를 선택하도록 하는 의문문으로 접속사 or를 쓴다.

Is she happy **or** sad? – Happy. 그녀는 / 즐겁니 / 아니면 / 슬프니? – 즐거워.

Which do you like better, spring **or** fall?
– I like spring better.
봄과 / 가을 중 / 어느 것을 / 더 / 좋아해? – 봄을 / 더 / 좋아해.

형태	동사+주어 ~ A or B?
	의문사+동사+주어, ~ A or B?
Yes/No로 대답하지 않는다.	

GRAMMAR CHECK

우리말에 맞게 빈칸에 알맞은 말을 쓰시오.

1. 너는 / 배고프지, 그렇지 / 않니?
   You are hungry, __________ __________ ?
2. Steve는 / 답을 / 알지 / 못하지, 그렇지?
   Steve doesn't know the answer, __________ __________ ?
3. 일찍 / 잠자리에 들어라, 알았지?
   Go to bed early, __________ __________ ?
4. 교실을 / 청소하자, 그럴 거지?
   Let's clean the classroom, __________ __________ ?
5. Smith 씨는 / 미국 사람이니 / 아니면 / 캐나다 사람이니?
   Is Mr. Smith from the USA __________ Canada?
6. 너와 / 네 언니 중 / 누가 / 샌드위치를 / 만들었니?
   __________ made sandwiches, you __________ your sister?

01 다음 문장을 부가의문문으로 바꾸어 쓰시오.

1. It is a nice day.

____

2. Computers work fast.

____

3. You can't play the violin.

____

4. You and Tom aren't in the same class.

____

5. Be a good boy.

____

6. Let's go to the movies.

____

02 틀린 부분을 바르게 고쳐 문장을 다시 쓰시오.

1. She is your English teacher, is not she?

____

2. Calvin can drive a car, can't Calvin?

____

3. Let's join our school band, will you?

____

4. Don't be noisy in the library, do you?

____

5. How do you go there, by bus and by train?

____

6. Allan wasn't in Paris last week, did he?

____

03 주어진 단어를 사용하여 우리말에 맞게 문장을 쓰시오.

1. 너는 수영을 못하지, 그렇지? (swim)

____

2. 에펠 탑은 프랑스에 있어, 그렇지 않니? (in France, the Eiffel Tower)

____

3. 그녀는 책을 읽고 있니 아니면 편지를 읽고 있니? (read, a letter, a book)

____

4. 이 책상을 옮기자, 그럴 거지? (move)

____

5. 그는 피자와 파스타 중 어느 것을 더 좋아하니? (better, pasta)

____

6. 집에 오는 길에 우유를 사, 그럴 거지? (on your way home)

____

통합 서술형

● 두 사람이 주문한 메뉴를 보고 다음 대화를 완성하시오.

	Jane	Mike
(soup)	V	V
(steak)		V
(spaghetti)	V	
(coffee)		
(juice)		V

Jane: Mike, pass me the menu, __________ __________?

Mike: Here you are.

Jane: Let's eat corn soup, __________ __________?

Mike: OK. Then __________ do you like better, steak __________ spaghetti?

Jane: I like __________ better. What about you?

Mike: I want __________. I also want some coffee.

Jane: You already drank two cups of coffee. Don't drink any more coffee, __________ __________?

Mike: Then I'll drink __________.

Chapter

08

to부정사

CORE 22 명사적 용법

CORE 23 형용사적 용법

CORE 24 부사적 용법

CORE 22 명사적 용법

- to부정사(to+동사원형)는 명사처럼 주어, 보어, 목적어로 쓰일 수 있다.

To read novels is interesting. <주어> 소설을 / 읽는 것은 / 흥미롭다.

= It is interesting **to read** novels.
가주어 진주어

My dream is **to become** a scientist. <보어>
나의 꿈은 / 과학자가 되는 것이다.

He wanted **to drink** orange juice. <목적어>
그는 / 오렌지 주스를 / 마시기를 / 원했다.

명사적 용법(~하는 것, ~하기)	
주어	To부정사+동사 ~. = It(가주어) ~ to부정사(진주어) ...
보어	주어+be동사+to부정사 ~.
목적어	주어+동사+to부정사 ~.

GRAMMAR CHECK

밑줄 친 to부정사의 역할을 <보기>에서 찾아 쓰시오.

보기 주어 보어 목적어

1. To grow plants is not easy. ________
2. We decided to take a train. ________
3. To have a dream is important. ________
4. Her job is to teach children. ________
5. They like to go to the mountains. ________
6. My plan is to exercise every day. ________
7. Chris hopes to buy a backpack. ________

NOTE

to부정사를 목적어로 취하는 동사

agree	begin	decide	expect
fail	hope	like	love
start	plan	want	wish

Check 주어진 단어를 빈칸에 적절한 형태로 써넣으시오.

1. Dad loves ________ with me. (talk)
2. I began ________ Chinese. (learn)
3. We expected ________ the game. (win)

01

주어진 단어를 바르게 배열하여 우리말에 맞게 문장을 완성하시오.

1. 계획을 세우는 것은 필수적이다. (make, a plan, is, to)
   ______________________ necessary.
2. 나의 언니는 프랑스 음식 먹는 것을 좋아한다. (to, loves, French food, eat)
   My sister ______________________ .
3. Judy의 꿈은 세계를 여행하는 것이다. (travel, is, to, the world)
   Judy's dream ______________________ .
4. 외국 친구들을 만드는 것은 흥미롭다. (to, interesting, make, is, foreign friends)
   It ______________________ .
5. 그들은 박물관을 방문하기로 계획했다. (visit, planned, to, the museum)
   They ______________________ .
6. 그의 직업은 사과 나무를 키우는 것이다. (to, grow, apple trees, is)
   His job ______________________ .

02

틀린 부분을 바르게 고쳐 문장을 다시 쓰시오.

1. Learn taekwondo is very exciting.
   ____
2. It is fun run on the beach.
   ____
3. Jenny likes draw pictures.
   ____
4. Eric's hope is become a singer.
   ____
5. They expected seeing her again.
   ____
6. That is impossible finished the work in a week.
   ____

03 주어진 단어를 사용하여 우리말에 맞게 문장을 완성하시오.

1. 야구를 하는 것은 신난다. (play, baseball)

   ______________________ exciting.

2. 엄마는 집을 청소하기 시작하셨다. (start, clean, the house)

   Mom ______________________.

3. Emily의 취미는 자전거를 타는 것이다. (ride, a bike)

   Emily's hobby ______________________.

4. 체중을 줄이는 것은 쉽지 않다. (easy, lose)

   ______________________ weight.

5. 그는 예약을 하는 데 실패했다. (fail, make, a reservation)

   He ______________________.

6. 나의 목표는 내년에 학교를 마치는 것이다. (finish, school, next year)

   My goal ______________________.

7. 매일 일기를 쓰는 것은 중요하다. (write in, a diary, every day)

   ______________________ important.

통합 서술형

● Jack과 Mina를 소개한 표를 보고 아래 글을 완성하시오.

이름	Jack	Mina
좋아하는 것	cook food on weekends watch food shows on TV	go to the mountains with her dad take pictures of flowers
희망	become a cook	exhibit flower photos

I have two friends, Jack and Mina.

1. Jack likes ______________ on weekends.

   ______________ on TV is also his favorite.

   His hope is ______________.

2. Mina loves ______________ with her dad.

   She says, "It is exciting ______________ of flowers."

   Her dream is ______________.

CORE 23 형용사적 용법

● to부정사가 형용사처럼 (대)명사를 뒤에서 수식할 수 있다.

He had much work to finish.

그는 / 끝내야 할 / 많은 일이 / 있었다.

Sara needs someone to talk with.

Sara는 / 함께 / 이야기할 / 누군가가 / 필요하다.

Dad wanted something cold to drink.

아빠는 / 차가운 / 마실 / 무언가를 / 원하셨다.

명사+to부정사	a shirt to wash 세탁할 셔츠
명사+to부정사+전치사	a chair to sit on (위에) 앉을 의자
-thing/ -one/ -body +형용사+to부정사	something warm to wear 따뜻한 입을 무언가

GRAMMAR CHECK

주어진 단어를 바르게 배열하여 우리말에 맞게 문장을 완성하시오.

1. 읽어야 할 / 많은 책들이 / 있다. (to read, many books)

   There are ______________________.

2. 그들은 / 휴식을 취할 / 시간이 / 있었다. (to take, a break, time)

   They had ______________________.

3. 나는 / 쓸 / 색연필을 / 구입했다. (to write with, a colored pencil)

   I bought ______________________.

4. Diana는 / 너에게 / 해줄 / 재미있는 이야기가 / 있다. (funny stories, you, to tell)

   Diana has ______________________.

5. 그 여자는 / 그녀를 / 도와줄 / 누군가를 / 찾고 있다. (to help, her, someone)

   The woman is looking for ______________________.

6. June은 / 거주할 / 아파트가 / 필요하다. (to live in, an apartment)

   June needs ______________________.

7. 이번 주말에 / 할 / 특별한 / 무언가가 / 있나요? (this weekend, special, anything, to do)

   Is there ______________________?

01

주어진 단어를 사용하여 우리말에 맞게 문장을 완성하시오.

1. 그 학생들은 타야 할 기차가 있었다. (a train, catch)
   The students had ______________________________.

2. 함께 놀 누군가가 있었니? (with, anybody, play)
   Was there ______________________________?

3. Emma는 장난감들을 살 돈을 가지고 있지 않았다. (money, buy, toys)
   Emma didn't have ______________________________.

4. Susie는 머무를 호텔을 찾고 있다. (at, a hotel, stay)
   Susie is looking for ______________________________.

5. 그녀는 슈퍼마켓에 갈 시간이 없었다. (no time, go, to the supermarket)
   She had ______________________________.

6. 그 남자는 춤을 출 파트너가 필요했다. (with, a partner, dance)
   The man needed ______________________________.

7. 너는 기억할 중요한 무언가가 있니? (anything, important, remember)
   Do you have ______________________________?

02

밑줄 친 부분을 바르게 고쳐 문장을 다시 쓰시오.

1. Susan has a lot of heavy boxes move.
   ____

2. Please give me to read something.
   ____

3. Her grandparents built a new house to live.
   ____

4. Does Jimmy want sweet anything to eat?
   ____

5. I am looking for friends to play.
   ____

6. The children needed paper to write.
   ____

03 **그림과 주어진 단어를 사용하여 엄마와 Mary의 대화를 완성하시오.**

(1)

a book / read

(2)

something / sweet / eat

(3)

a puppy / play

Mom: Oh Mary, where did you go?

Mary: I went to the library, Mom.

I borrowed (1) ______________________________ .

Mom: Aren't you hungry?

Mary: Yes, I want (2) ______________________________ .

Mom: Eat some chocolate. It is on the table.

And what do you want for Christmas?

Mary: Can I have (3) ______________________________ ?

Mom: Well, I will talk about it with your dad.

Mary: Thanks, Mom.

통합 서술형

다음 표를 보고 주어진 단어를 사용하여 아래 글을 완성하시오.

이름	준비할 것
Eddy	vegetables
Jumi	something cold
Gabriel	birthday cards
Tommy	pretty paper

Tomorrow, Hana's friends will throw a surprise party for her.

Eddy will bring ______________________________ . (make salad)

Jumi will prepare ______________________________ . (drink)

Gabriel will make ______________________________ . (write)

Tommy will buy ______________________________ . (decorate)

CORE 24 부사적 용법

● to부정사는 부사처럼 동사, 형용사 등을 수식할 수 있다.

He studied hard **to pass** the test. <목적>
그는 / 시험을 / 통과하기 위해서 / 열심히 공부했다.

The woman was glad **to meet** my parents. <감정의 원인>
그 여자는 / 나의 부모님을 / 만나서 / 기뻤다.

She grew up **to become** a painter. <결과>
그녀는 / 자라서 / 화가가 / 되었다.

English is not easy **to learn**. <정도> 영어는 / 배우기에 / 쉽지 않다.

목적	~하기 위해서, ~하려 (= in order to+동사원형)
감정의 원인	~해서, ~하니 감정 형용사 glad, pleased, happy, surprised, upset, angry 등과 함께 쓰인다.
결과	~해서 (그 결과) …하다 grow up, live, awake up과 같은 동사와 자주 쓰인다.
정도	~하기(에)

GRAMMAR CHECK

주어진 동사를 사용하여 우리말에 맞게 문장을 완성하시오.

solve fail fight watch find buy

1. Thomas는 / 바지를 / 사기 위해서 / 쇼핑센터에 / 갔다.
   Thomas went to the shopping center ____________ pants.
2. 그 소녀는 / 시험에 실패해서 / 실망했다.
   The girl was disappointed ____________ the test.
3. Alex는 / 일어나보니 / 자신이 / 유명해져 있다는 것을 / 알았다.
   Alex awoke up ____________ himself famous.
4. 이 문제들은 / 풀기 / 어렵다.
   These problems are hard ____________ .
5. 아빠는 / 그 다큐멘터리를 / 보기 위해서 / 텔레비전을 / 켜셨다.
   Dad turned on the TV ____________ the documentary.
6. 그녀는 / 남동생들과 / 싸워서 / 속상했다.
   She was upset ____________ with her brothers.

01

밑줄 친 to부정사에 유의하여 다음 문장을 우리말로 옮기시오.

1. The woman exercises to lose weight.

   ____

2. I was surprised to see him.

   ____

3. The boy grew up to be a teacher.

   ____

4. This book is difficult to understand.

   ____

5. They went to the zoo to see pandas.

   ____

6. My grandmother lived to be 90 years old.

   ____

02

주어진 단어를 사용하여 우리말에 맞게 문장을 완성하시오.

1. Sera는 성공하기 위해서 열심히 일했다. (work, hard, succeed)

   Sera ______________________________ .

2. 이 호수는 측정하기에 깊다. (deep, measure)

   This lake ______________________________ .

3. 나는 그의 편지를 받고 기뻤다. (glad, receive, his letter)

   I ______________________________ .

4. 그 소년은 자라서 기타리스트가 되었다. (grow up, become, a guitarist)

   The boy ______________________________ .

5. 그는 저녁을 만들기 위해서 주방으로 갔다. (go, to the kitchen, make, dinner)

   He ______________________________ .

6. 그녀는 일어나보니 집에 혼자 있는 것을 알았다. (awake up, find herself, alone)

   She ______________________________ .

7. Harry는 그의 사촌들과 시간을 보내서 기뻤다. (pleased, spend, time, with his cousins)

   Harry ______________________________ .

03 표를 보고 Thomas Edison과 Marie Curie에 관한 아래 글을 완성하시오.

이름	Thomas Edison	Marie Curie
좋아하는 것	make new things	study physics
직업	become an inventor	become a scientist
주요 업적	invent light bulbs	find new materials

1. Thomas Edison was always happy ______________________.

   He grew up ______________________.

   He did experiments ______________________.

   He developed many devices and they greatly influenced life around the world.

2. Marie Curie was delighted ______________________.

   She grew up ______________________.

   She did her research ______________________.

   She was the first woman to win a Nobel Prize.

통합 서술형

● 다음 일기를 읽고 밑줄 친 문장의 틀린 부분을 바르게 고쳐 문장을 다시 쓰시오.

> My dream is to become a singer. So I decided to enter the song contest. (1) I practiced hard win the contest. (2) The contest was difficult win. (3) I was disappointed lost the contest. But I will never give up my dream. (4) I will grow up become a famous singer.

(1) ______________________

(2) ______________________

(3) ______________________

(4) ______________________

Chapter

09

동명사

CORE 25 동명사의 역할

CORE 26 동명사·to부정사를 목적어로 취하는 동사

CORE 25 동명사의 역할

동명사(동사원형+-ing)는 동사 역할을 하여 목적어를 취할 수 있으며, 명사처럼 문장 안에서 주어, 보어, 목적어로 쓰일 수 있다.

① 주어

Playing soccer is fun. 축구를 하는 것은 / 재미있다.
(soccer → 동명사 playing의 목적어)
= To play

② 보어

My hobby is cooking food. 나의 취미는 / 음식을 만드는 것이다.
= to cook

③ 목적어

I enjoy **riding** a bike. <동사의 목적어> 나는 / 자전거 타는 것을 / 즐긴다.

He is excited about **leaving** for Paris. <전치사의 목적어>
그는 / 파리로 떠나는 것에 / 들떠 있다

> 동명사는 avoid, enjoy, finish, practice, consider, stop 등과 같은 동사의 목적어로 쓰인다.

GRAMMAR CHECK 밑줄 친 동명사의 역할을 <보기>에서 찾아 쓰시오.

보기: 주어 보어 동사의 목적어 전치사의 목적어

1. Taking a walk is good for you. ________
2. Jack finished writing his essay. ________
3. Her dream is becoming a doctor. ________
4. Jessica is good at speaking Chinese. ________
5. Going to the theme park is exciting. ________

현재분사

현재분사는 명사를 수식하는 형용사 역할을 하며, be동사와 함께 현재진행형을 만든다.

The **swimming** fish is big.
그 헤엄치고 있는 물고기는 크다.

Jina is **swimming**. Jina는 수영을 하고 있다.

Check 밑줄 친 부분이 동명사인지 현재분사인지 쓰시오.

1. My plan is exercising every day. ________
2. He is running now. ________
3. I saw a crying baby. ________
4. Eating fruit is good for you. ________

01 주어진 단어를 바르게 배열하여 우리말에 맞게 문장을 완성하시오.

1. 생물학을 공부하는 것은 무척 흥미롭다. (studying, is, biology)
   ______________________ very interesting.

2. Thomas의 가족은 태국 음식 먹기를 즐긴다. (enjoys, eating, Thai food)
   Thomas' family ______________________.

3. 엄마의 취미는 골프를 치는 것이다. (playing, golf, is)
   Mom's hobby ______________________.

4. 약속을 지키는 것은 중요하다. (your promises, keeping, is)
   ______________________ important.

5. 그 여자는 시험을 통과한 것이 자랑스러웠다. (the exam, passing, was proud of)
   The woman ______________________.

6. 우리의 계획은 이번 여름에 알프스 산을 오르는 것이다. (the Alps, climbing, this summer, is)
   Our plan ______________________.

02 틀린 부분을 바르게 고쳐 문장을 다시 쓰시오.

1. Play basketball with friends is fun.
   ____

2. Does Emma enjoy grow plants and flowers?
   ____

3. The girl's habit is bite her nails.
   ____

4. I am afraid of ride a bike.
   ____

5. He practiced drive a car.
   ____

6. They are not excited about to watch a movie.
   ____

03 주어진 단어를 사용하여 우리말에 맞게 문장을 완성하시오.

1. 그녀는 소설을 쓰는 것에 관심이 있다. (be interested in, write, novels)
   She ______________________________ .

2. 그 학생들은 테니스 클럽을 만드는 것을 고려한다. (consider, a tennis club, form)
   The students ______________________________ .

3. 지하철을 타는 것이 차를 운전하는 것보다 빠르다. (take, the subway, faster)
   ______________________________ than driving a car.

4. 나의 직업은 여성 의류를 디자인하는 것이다. (women's clothes, design)
   My job ______________________________ .

5. 나의 이모는 쿠키를 굽는 것을 좋아하신다. (be fond of, bake, cookies)
   My aunt ______________________________ .

6. 밤에 별들을 보는 것은 흥미롭다. (look at, the stars, at night)
   ______________________________ interesting.

7. 그는 버스에서 휴대전화 사용하는 것을 피한다. (avoid, use, his cell phone, on the bus)
   He ______________________________ .

통합 서술형

● 표를 보고 아래 글을 완성하시오.

	pandas	elephants
좋아하는 것	eat bamboo leaves	eat leaves and fruit
잘하는 것	climb trees	catch things with their nose
습성	rest during the day	take a mud shower

1. Pandas enjoy ______________________________ in the woods.
   They are good at ______________________________ .
   Their habit is ______________________________ .

2. Elephants like ______________________________ .
   They are good at ______________________________ .
   ______________________________ is their habit.

CORE 26 동명사·to부정사를 목적어로 취하는 동사

1 동명사만 목적어로 취하는 동사: admit, enjoy, mind, finish, quit, keep, practice, stop 등

He admitted lying to me. 그는 / 나에게 / 거짓말 한 것을 / 인정했다.

Tom stopped talking on the cell phone. Tom은 / 휴대전화로 / 이야기하는 것을 / 멈췄다.

cf. stop+to부정사: ~하기 위해서 멈추다(부사적 용법-목적)

Tom **stopped to talk** on the cell phone. Tom은 / 휴대전화로 / 이야기하기 위해서 / 멈췄다.

2 to부정사만 목적어로 취하는 동사: agree, decide, hope, expect, learn, plan, promise, refuse 등

She decided to quit her work. 그녀는 / 자신의 일을 / 그만두기로 / 결정했다.

3 동명사와 to부정사 모두를 목적어로 취하는 동사: like, love, start, begin, continue 등은 의미 변화가 없으나 forget, remember, try의 경우 의미 변화가 있다.

forget/remember
- 동명사: (과거에) ~했던 것을 잊다/기억하다
- to부정사: (미래에) ~할 것을 잊다/기억하다

try
- 동명사: ~을 시험 삼아 해보다
- to부정사: ~하려고 노력하다

I will not forget meeting her. 나는 / 그녀를 / 만났던 것을 / 잊지 못할 것이다.

Don't forget to meet Jim tomorrow. 내일 / Jim을 / 만날 것을 / 잊지 말아라.

GRAMMAR CHECK

우리말에 맞게 주어진 동사의 알맞은 형태를 써넣어 문장을 완성하시오.

1. 그 어린이들은 / 다 함께 / 노래 부르는 것을 / 즐겼다. (sing)
   The children enjoyed ______________ all together.
2. Jack은 / 만화 캐릭터 그리는 것을 / 좋아한다. (draw)
   Jack loves ______________ cartoon characters.
3. 그녀는 / 선물을 받는 것을 / 기대했다. (receive)
   She expected ______________ a present.
4. 언니는 / 바이올린 연습을 / 시작할 것이다. (practice)
   My sister will begin ______________ the violin.
5. 제가 / 문을 / 닫아도 될까요? (close)
   Would you mind ______________ the door?
6. Chris는 / 새 집을 / 짓는 데 / 동의했다. (build)
   Chris agreed ______________ a new house.

01

틀린 부분을 바르게 고쳐 문장을 다시 쓰시오.

1. I finished to answer all his questions.

____

2. The actor hoped receiving the award.

____

3. The boys started watch the soccer game.

____

4. Will the company keep to produce computers?

____

5. My brother promised going to the dentist.

____

02

주어진 단어를 사용하여 우리말에 맞게 문장을 완성하시오.

1. 나는 문을 잠갔던 것을 기억한다. (remember, the door, lock)
I ______________________________ .

2. 너는 그 소포를 보낼 것을 기억해야 한다. (post, remember, the package)
You should ______________________________ .

3. 그녀는 그 문제를 해결하려고 노력했다. (tried, solve, the problem)
She ______________________________ .

4. 형은 연을 시험 삼아 만들어 보았다. (tried, kites, make)
My brother ______________________________ .

5. 그 책을 반납할 것을 잊지 마세요. (return, forget)
______________________________ the book.

6. 그는 Emily를 보았던 것을 잊지 않을 것이다. (forget, see)
He will not ______________________________ .

7. Henry는 나와 이야기하기 위해 멈췄다. (stopped, me, talk with)
Henry ______________________________ .

8. 그 남자는 신문을 읽는 것을 멈췄다. (read, stopped, the newspaper)
The man ______________________________ .

03 주어진 단어를 사용하여 우리말에 맞게 아래 글을 완성하시오.

오늘 나는 런던에 사는 사촌에게서 이메일을 받았다.
그는 빅 벤 사진도 보내왔다.
문득 작년 여름에 템스 강을 따라 걸었던 게 기억났다.
그때 나는 런던 관광을 무척 즐겼다.
다시 런던에 가게 되기를 기대하며 잠자리에 들어야겠다.
내일 사촌에게 답장 쓰는 것을 잊지 말아야겠다.

Today I got an e-mail from my cousin in London.
He also sent a photo of Big Ben.
Suddenly I remembered ________ along the Thames last summer. (walk)
At that time I enjoyed ________ London very much. (see)
I hope ________ London again, and now I will go to bed. (visit)
Tomorrow, I will never forget ________ his e-mail. (answer)

통합서술형

● 주어진 단어를 사용하여 그림을 설명하는 글을 완성하시오.

Tina's family went to Paris last summer.
Mom loved ____________ in a café. (drink coffee)
Dad planned ____________ of the city. (take pictures)
Tina stopped ____________ with people. (speak French)
Tina's brother kept ____________ . (walk along the streets)

Chapter 10

전치사와 접속사

CORE 27 전치사

CORE 28 등위접속사

CORE 29 명사절을 이끄는 접속사 that

CORE 30 부사절을 이끄는 접속사

CORE 27 전치사

1 시간 전치사: 시간이나 때를 나타내는 명사(구) 앞에 쓴다.

The festival started **at** 6 o'clock **on** May 24th **in** 2015.
축제는 / 2015년 / 5월 24일 / 6시에 / 시작했다.

He practiced Chinese **for** two hours **during** the vacation.
그는 / 방학 / 2시간 동안 / 중국어를 / 연습했다.

Come back **by** 5. I will wait **until** 5.
5시까지 / 돌아와. 내가 / 5시까지 / 기다릴게.

She left **before** breakfast and I arrived **after** dinner. 그녀는 / 아침 전에 / 떠났고, 나는 / 점심 후에 / 도착했다.

at / on / in	
at	+ 시각, 특정 시점
on	+ 날짜, 요일, 특정한 날
in	+ 월, 계절, 연도 / 하루의 때
기타 시간 전치사	

for + 숫자 기간 / during + 특정 기간] ~ 동안
by ~까지(완료) / until ~까지(계속)
after ~후에 / before ~ 전에

2 장소 전치사: 위치나 장소를 나타내는 명사(구) 앞에 쓴다.

He works **at** the drugstore **in** the country.
그는 / 시골에 있는 / 약국에서 / 일한다.

The ships and boats are **under** the bridge.
배와 보트가 / 다리 밑에 / 있다.

at / in / on	
at	+ 좁은 장소나 하나의 지점
in	+ 도시, 국가 등 넓은 장소나 내부
on	+ 표면에 접촉한 상태
기타 장소 전치사	

under ~ 아래(밑)에 ↔ over ~ 위에
in front of ~ 앞에 ↔ behind ~뒤에

GRAMMAR CHECK

우리말에 맞게 둘 중에서 어법에 맞는 것을 고르시오.

1. 그는 / 보통 / 6시에 / 일어난다. → He usually gets up (on / at) six o'clock.
2. Ed는 / 여행 하는 동안 / 그 선물을 샀다. → Ed bought the gift (for / during) the trip.
3. 벽 위에 있는 / 사진을 / 보아라. → Look at the picture (over / on) the wall.
4. Jasmine은 / 캐나다에 / 살았나요? → Did Jasmine live (in / on) Canada?
5. 상점 앞에 / 차 한 대가 / 있다. → There is a car (behind / in front of) the store.

방향을 나타내는 전치사

to	~로	for	~을 향하여
into	~ 안으로	out of	~ 밖으로
up	~ 위로	down	~ 아래로
along	~을 따라서	across	~을 가로질러

Check 빈칸에 알맞은 전치사를 쓰시오.

1. 상자 밖으로 → ________ the box
2. 런던을 향하여 → ________ London
3. 사막을 가로질러 → ________ the desert

01 우리말에 맞게 빈칸에 알맞은 전치사를 쓰시오.

1. 그들은 봄에 그 영화를 보았다.
   They watched the movie __________ spring.

2. 우리는 설날에 한복을 입는다.
   We wear *hanbok* __________ New Year's Day.

3. Susan은 방과 후에 바이올린을 연습하니?
   Does Susan practice the violin __________ school?

4. 형은 저녁을 먹기 전에 집을 떠났다.
   My brother left home __________ dinner.

5. 기차는 저녁 5시에 출발했다.
   The train started __________ five o'clock __________ the evening.

6. 일요일 아침에 여기서 만나자.
   Let's meet here __________ Sunday morning.

02 전치사와 주어진 단어를 사용하여 우리말에 맞게 문장을 완성하시오.

1. 그는 건물 뒤에 주차했다. (the building)
   He parked his car ____________________________________.

2. 그는 1시간 동안 노래를 부르고 있다. (one hour)
   He is singing ____________________________________.

3. Sandra는 철길을 따라 뛰었다. (the railroad tracks)
   Sandra ran ____________________________________.

4. 산 위에 무지개가 보이니? (the mountain)
   Can you see the rainbow ____________________________________?

5. 그 식당은 10시까지 문을 연다. (ten o'clock)
   The restaurant stays open ____________________________________.

6. 소년은 계단을 올라가고 있고, 소녀는 계단을 내려가고 있다. (the stairs)
   The boy is walking ______________, and the girl is walking ______________.

03 틀린 부분을 모두 바르게 고쳐 문장을 다시 쓰시오.

1. There is a family picture at the wall.

____

2. Kelly studied for her test during three hours.

____

3. The swimming pool is in front the hotel.

____

4. I have breakfast in 7 o'clock on the morning.

____

5. Laura lived at France on 2008.

____

6. Paul will leave to New York in September 26th.

____

통합 서술형

◉ 다음 그림과 일치하도록 알맞은 전치사를 넣어 글을 완성하시오.

There are many people in the park __________ the afternoon.
Some people are jogging __________ the road.
Birds are flying __________ the tree, and children are playing __________ the tree.
Two people are sitting __________ the bench __________ the tree.

CORE 28 등위접속사

대등한 단어와 단어, 구와 구, 절과 절을 연결할 때 등위접속사를 쓴다.

and	비슷한 내용 연결 (그리고, ~와)
but	반대되는 내용 연결 (그러나, 하지만)
or	둘 중에서 선택 (또는, 아니면)
so	앞 일의 결과 (그래서, 그러므로)

I bought bread and milk. (단어+단어)
나는 / 빵과 / 우유를 / 샀다.

My grandmother is old but healthy. (단어+단어)
할머니는 / 연세가 많으시지만 / 건강하시다.

Do you go to school by bus or on foot? (구+구) 학교에 / 버스를 타고 가니 / 아니면 / 걸어서 가니?

It was very hot, so we opened the window. (절+절) 날씨가 / 아주 더워서 / 우리는 / 창문을 / 열었다.

GRAMMAR CHECK

우리말에 맞게 둘 중에서 어법에 맞는 것을 고르시오.

1. Bill과 / Judy는 / 좋은 / 친구이다.
   Bill (and / or) Judy are good friends.
2. Victoria는 / 예쁘지만 / 불친절하다.
   Victoria is pretty (so / but) unfriendly.
3. 너는 / 주스 / 또는 / 우유 중에서 / 어떤 것을 / 더 / 좋아하니?
   Which do you like better, juice (or / and) milk?
4. 그녀는 / 늦게 / 일어나서 / 열차를 / 놓쳤다.
   She got up late, (but / so) she missed the train.
5. 우체국은 / 오른쪽에 / 있나요 / 아니면 / 왼쪽에 / 있나요?
   Is the post office on the right (or / but) on the left?

「명령문+and」와 「명령문+or」

- 명령문+and: ~해라, 그러면
  Try hard, and you can succeed.
  열심히 노력해라, 그러면 성공할 수 있다.
- 명령문+or: ~해라, 그렇지 않으면
  Hurry up, or you'll be late for school.
  서둘러라, 그렇지 않으면 학교에 지각할 것이다.

Check 빈칸에 and와 or 중에서 골라 쓰시오.

1. Be careful, ________ you will hurt.
2. Exercise ever day, ________ you'll get healthy.
3. Hurry up, ________ you can get there on time.
4. Tell me everything, ________ I can't help you.

01 우리말에 맞게 빈칸에 알맞은 접속사를 쓰시오.

1. 그 소설은 길지만 재미있다.
   The novel is long ______________ interesting.

2. Jack은 자신의 컴퓨터와 휴대전화를 가지고 싶어 한다.
   Jack wants to have his own computer ______________ cell phone.

3. Clara는 아파서 일찍 잠자리에 들었다.
   Clara was sick, ______________ she went to bed early.

4. 나는 버스 아니면 지하철로 학교에 간다.
   I go to school by bus ______________ by subway.

5. 모퉁이에서 왼쪽으로 도세요, 그러면 식당을 발견할 수 있을 겁니다.
   Turn left at the corner, ______________ you can find the restaurant.

6. 스웨터를 입어라, 그렇지 않으면 감기에 걸릴 것이다.
   Wear the sweater, ______________ you will catch a cold.

02 등위접속사와 주어진 단어를 사용하여 우리말에 맞게 문장을 완성하시오.

1. 나는 연필 한 자루와 공책 한 권이 필요하다. (a pencil, a notebook)
   I need ______________________________________ .

2. 그 수프는 차지만 맛있다. (cold, tasty)
   The soup is ______________________________________ .

3. 날씨가 맑아서 우리는 산책을 한다. (go for a walk)
   The weather is fine, ______________________________________ .

4. 너는 영화를 봤니 아니면 집에 있었니? (go to the movies, stay at home)
   Did you ______________________________________ ?

5. 그 버튼을 눌러라, 그러면 문이 열릴 것이다. (open)
   Press the button, ______________________________________ .

6. 지금 일어나라, 그렇지 않으면 기차를 놓칠 것이다. (miss the train)
   Get up now, ______________________________________ .

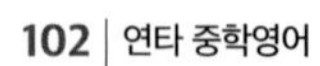

03 틀린 부분을 바르게 고쳐 문장을 다시 쓰시오.

1. Samantha has many caps but hats.

____

2. Would you like to pay in cash and by card?

____

3. Tom can speak English, and he can't speak Korean.

____

4. He spoke loudly, but everyone could hear him well.

____

5. Do it right now, and you will not finish it.

____

6. Study hard, or you can get a good grade.

____

통합 서술형

다음 문자 메시지를 읽고 우리말에 맞게 문장을 쓰시오.

Hi, David. This is Clara.
(1) Sally와 나는 내일 영화 보러 갈 거야.
Will you join us?
(2) 나는 액션 영화를 좋아하지만 Sally는 좋아하지 않아. (action movies)
She likes horror movies.
(3) 넌 액션 영화와 공포 영화 중 어떤 것을 더 좋아하니? (which, better)
(4) 내게 전화해, 그러면 이에 대해 더 얘기할 수 있을 거야. (call, more, about)

(1) ______________________________
(2) ______________________________
(3) ______________________________
(4) ______________________________

CORE 29 명사절을 이끄는 접속사 that

접속사 that은 '~하는 것'이라는 뜻으로 문장에서 주어, 목적어, 보어 역할을 하는 명사절을 이끈다.

1. 주어 역할: 「It~ that절」 문장으로 바꾸어 쓸 수 있다.

That Mt. Everest is the highest mountain in the world is true.

= It is true that Mt. Everest is the highest mountain in the world.

가주어 진주어

에베레스트 산이 / 세계에서 / 가장 높은 산이라는 것은 / 사실이다.

2. 목적어 역할: that은 생략할 수 있다.

I hope (that) your parents will get well soon. 너의 부모님께서 / 어서 / 회복되기를 / 희망한다.

3. 보어 역할

The fact is that he passed the difficult exam. 사실은 / 그가 / 그 어려운 시험에 / 합격했다는 / 것이다.

GRAMMAR CHECK

1 밑줄 친 that절의 역할이 주어, 보어, 목적어 중에서 무엇인지 쓰시오.

1. That Samantha is a good cook is true. ____________
2. Her dream is that she will be a famous doctor. ____________
3. I hope that I'll become a pianist. ____________
4. It is strange that Emily didn't come to my party. ____________

2 보기와 같이 접속사 that이 들어갈 자리에 √ 표시 하시오.

보기 I think √ the Italian restaurant is good.

1. I think you and your brother are very kind.
2. The point is we don't have enough time.
3. It is certain he will come back home tomorrow.
4. The problem is I don't know his phone number.

01 다음 두 문장을 접속사를 사용하여 한 문장으로 고쳐 쓰시오.

1. I hope. She'll become a history teacher.

   I hope ______________________________.

2. It is very strange. He arrived there on time.

   It is very strange ______________________________.

3. I know. Dick will go to Seoul tomorrow.

   I know ______________________________.

4. It is possible. Max finishes the work in 2 hours.

   It ______________________________.

5. I believe. Dave will pass the entrance exam.

   I believe ______________________________.

02 주어진 단어를 바르게 배열하여 우리말에 맞게 문장을 완성하시오.

1. 나는 네가 좋은 친구라고 생각한다.

   (that, are, I, think, you)

   ______________________________ a good friend.

2. 내 소망은 올 여름에 수영을 할 수 있는 것이다.

   (I, that, can swim, my hope, is)

   ______________________________ this summer.

3. Steve가 캐나다로 갈 것이라는 것은 확실하다.

   (Steve, it, certain, is, that, will go)

   ______________________________ to Canada.

4. 좋은 소식은 그가 금메달을 땄다는 것이다.

   (the good news, he, that, won, is)

   ______________________________ the gold medal.

5. 그녀가 5개 국어를 할 수 있다는 것은 놀랍다.

   (is, it, surprising, that, can speak, she)

   ______________________________ five languages.

03 주어진 단어를 사용하여 우리말에 맞게 문장을 완성하시오.

1.

그 의사는 내가 감기에 걸렸다고 말했다. (had a cold)

The doctor ____________________.

2.

Jane은 그 이야기가 재미있다고 생각한다. (fun)

Jane ____________________.

3.

그녀가 A를 받았다는 것은 사실이다. (got an A)

It ____________________.

4.

내 희망은 선생님이 되는 것이다. (a teacher)

My hope ____________________.

통합 서술형

접속사와 (A)와 (B)의 표현을 한 번씩만 사용하여 아래 글을 완성하시오.

내 꿈은 과학자가 되는 것이다.
오늘 나는 퀴리 부인이 라듐을 발견했다고 배웠다.
퀴리 부인이 어려운 환경에서도 열심히 연구했다니 놀랍다.
나는 이제부터 열심히 공부하기로 결심했다.

보기 My dream is that I'll be a scientist.

(1) ____________________

(2) ____________________

I decided to study hard from now.

(A)	(B)
· It is surprising	· I'll be a scientist
· Today I learned	· Madame Curie discovered radium
· My dream is	· Madame Curie studied hard under hard conditions

CORE 30 부사절을 이끄는 접속사

① 시간을 나타내는 접속사

When I was young, my family lived in Busan.

내가 / 어렸을 / 때 / 우리 가족은 / 부산에서 / 살았다.

While Mr. Brown was cooking, Paul helped him.

Brown 씨가 / 요리를 하는 / 동안 / Paul은 / 그를 / 도왔다.

Judy will be a teacher **after** she graduates from college.

Judy는 / 대학을 / 졸업한 / 후에 / 선생님이 / 될 것이다. will graduate (X)

when	~할 때
while	~하는 동안
before	~하기 전에
after	~한 후에

시간과 조건의 부사절 내에서는 현재시제가 미래시제를 대신한다.

② 이유를 나타내는 접속사

I like the movie **because〔since/as〕** it is exciting.

나는 / 영화가 / 재미있기 / 때문에 / 좋아한다.

because	~하기 때문에, ~이므로
as	
since	

because+절 / because of+명사(구)

③ 조건을 나타내는 접속사

If it is fine tomorrow, we'll go on a picnic. 만약 / 내일 / 날씨가 / 맑으면 / 우리는 / 소풍을 / 갈 것이다.

Let's walk **unless** it's far from here.

= if it's not far from here

만약 / 여기에서 / 멀지 않다면 / 걸어가자.

if	만약 ~라면
unless	만약 ~하지 않는다면 (=if ~ not)

GRAMMAR CHECK

우리말에 맞게 둘 중에서 어법에 맞는 것을 고르시오.

1. Jack은 / 저녁 식사를 하기 / 전에 / 숙제를 / 했다.
   Jack did his homework (before / since) he had dinner.
2. 만약 / 주말에 / 눈이 오면 / 우리는 / 스키를 타러 / 갈 것이다.
   We'll go skiing (unless / if) it snows on the weekend.
3. 만약 / 당신에게 / 더 좋은 방안이 / 없다면 / 우리는 / 이 프로젝트를 / 실행할 것이다.
   (Unless / If) you have a better plan, we'll perform the project.
4. 나는 / 학교 버스를 / 놓쳤기 / 때문에 / 학교에 / 지각했다.
   I was late for school (after / because) I missed the school bus.
5. 안개 / 때문에 / 오늘 아침에 / 교통 사고가 / 있었다.
   (Because of / Because) the fog, there was a traffic accident this morning.

01 우리말에 맞게 빈칸에 알맞은 접속사를 쓰시오.

1. 나는 런던에 있을 때 Big Ben을 보았다.
   I saw Big Ben ________________ I was in London.

2. Mike가 거짓말을 했기 때문에 Mike의 엄마는 화가 나셨다.
   Mike's mom was angry ________________ Mike told a lie to her.

3. 만약 휴대전화가 있다면 좀 빌려 줄래요?
   ________________ you have a cell phone, can you lend it to me?

4. 그 소녀는 15살이 되기 전에 대단한 음악가가 될 것이다.
   ________________ the girl is 15 years old, she will be a great musician.

5. 그는 파리에 있는 동안 John을 만났다.
   He met John ________________ he was in Paris.

6. 만약 네가 도와줄 수 없다면 나는 Mary에게 부탁할 것이다.
   ________________ you can help me, I'll ask Mary for help.

02 두 문장의 의미가 같도록 빈칸에 알맞은 말을 쓰시오.

1. The party started before Mr. Brown came.
   = Mr. Brown came ________________ the party started.

2. Cathy was sick, so she was absent from school.
   = ________________ Cathy was sick, she was absent from school.

3. I will go for a walk if I am not sick.
   = I will go for a walk ________________ I am sick.

4. Get some rest and you'll get better soon.
   = ________________ you get some rest, you'll get better soon.

5. The train didn't leave on time because it rained.
   = The train didn't leave on time ________________ the rain.

03 접속사와 주어진 단어를 사용하여 우리말에 맞게 문장을 완성하시오.

1. 나는 피곤했기 때문에 일찍 집에 왔다. (tired)
   I came home early ______________________ .
2. 만약 저의 도움이 필요하면 제게 이메일을 보내 주세요. (my help)
   Please send me an e-mail ______________________ .
3. 엄마가 외출하신 동안 나는 남동생을 돌보았다. (out)
   ______________________ , I took care of my little brother.
4. 만약 바쁘지 않다면 나 좀 도와줄 수 있니? (busy)
   Can you help me ______________________ ?
5. 여행을 하기 전에 인터넷을 검색해 보아라. (take a trip)
   Please do some research on the Internet ______________________ .

통합 서술형

다음 하루 일과표의 내용과 일치하도록 알맞은 접속사를 넣어 일기를 완성하시오.

	My Daily Life
7:30 a.m.	get up
8:00 a.m.	eat breakfast
8:30 a.m.	go to school
3:00 p.m.	meet Kevin (promise to go skiing on Sunday if doesn't rain)
4:00 p.m.	come back home
6:00 p.m.	study math because I have an exam tomorrow
11:00 p.m.	write in my diary / listen to music

I got up at 7:30 in the morning.
I went to school ______________ I ate breakfast.
I met Kevin ______________ I came back home.
We'll go skiing on Sunday ______________ it rains.
I have an exam tomorrow, ______________ I studied math.
Now I'm writing in my diary ______________ I'm listening to music.

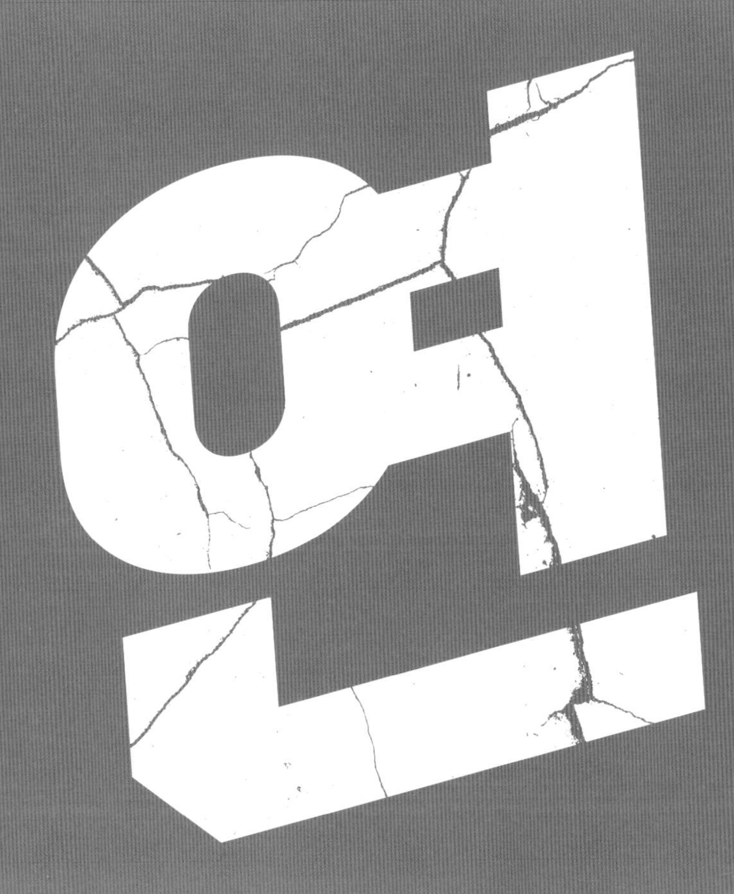

한 권으로
문법과 쓰기를
연속으로
타파!

포인트 30개로 중학영어 문법 · 쓰기 마스터

중학영어 문법+쓰기

중학 필수 문법 포인트 정리 | 문법 포인트에 기초한 체계적인 문장 쓰기 | 내신 서술형 평가 완벽 대비

LEVEL 1

정답 및 해설

YBM

중학영어 문법+쓰기

CHAPTER 01 be동사와 일반동사

CORE 01 be동사와 일반동사

Grammar Check p.8

1. am 2. are 3. is
4. lives 5. goes 6. studies

Check

1. you 2. they 3. we 4. she

01 p.9

1. is 2. am 3. is 4. is
5. are 6. are 7. are

02

1. comes 2. watches 3. has 4. cries
5. finishes 6. does 7. teaches

03 p.10

1. gets up 2. has breakfast
3. goes to school 4. studies Korean
5. writes in her diary

통합서술형

is, is, sings, is, takes, is, teaches, are

해석 | 내 이름은 민호다. 우리 가족은 대가족이다. 할머니께서는 노래를 잘 부르시는데 종종 재미있는 노래를 부르신다. 아버지는 의사이시므로 환자를 돌보신다. 어머니는 선생님이시고 학교에서 수학을 가르치신다. 남동생과 나는 학생이고 같은 학교에 다닌다.

CORE 02 be동사 부정문과 일반동사 부정문

Grammar Check p.11

1. It is not(isn't) delicious.
2. We are not(aren't) hungry now.
3. They do not(don't) get up early.
4. James does not(doesn't) know the answer.
5. He is not(isn't) a member of the club.
6. She does not(doesn't) like sandwiches.
7. The dog and the cat are not(aren't) on the bed.

01 p.12

1. I am not busy today.
   be동사의 부정문은 be동사 뒤에 not을 쓴다.
2. They do not play computer games.
   주어가 3인칭 복수일 때 일반동사의 부정형은 do not이다.
3. The story isn't funny to me.
   3인칭 단수의 부정 축약형은 isn't를 써야 한다.
4. You do not understand my feelings.
   일반동사의 부정문은 일반동사의 원형 앞에 do/does not을 쓴다.
5. Her uncle doesn't go to the beach.
   3인칭 단수의 부정문은 does not(doesn't)+동사원형이다
6. Elizabeth doesn't like meat or fish.
   3인칭 단수의 부정문이므로 doesn't 다음에 동사원형을 쓴다.

02

1. is not(isn't) cold
2. You are not(aren't) my neighbor
3. He does not(doesn't) hunt
4. My sister does not(doesn't) watch cartoons
5. Jane and I are not(aren't) at the ballpark
6. Bill and his brother do not(don't) listen to

03 p.13

1. does not(doesn't) play
2. am not
3. does not(doesn't) have

통합서술형

1. does not(doesn't) play
2. do not(don't) drink
3. They are not(aren't)
4. She does not(doesn't)
5. We do not(don't) like

CORE 03 be동사 의문문과 일반동사 의문문

Grammar Check p.14

1. Are you tired?
2. Is the car expensive?
3. Do they go to the museum?
4. Do we need a pet?
5. Am I late for school?
6. Does he speak French well?

01 p.15

1. Are you a middle school student?
2. Is Mr. Brown a doctor?
3. Are Tom and Mary
4. Do you learn Chinese
5. Does he go to the movies
6. Does Annie have a cell phone

02

1. Yes, I am.
2. No, she doesn't.
3. Is the bag expensive?
4. Do you drink milk?
5. Am I late for school?
   Yes, you are.
6. Does Andy teach math?
   No, he doesn't.

03 p.16

1. Does she like roses?
   주어가 3인칭 단수일 때 일반동사의 부정문은 「Does+주어+동사원형」이다.
2. Is Paul a farmer?
   Paul이 농부냐고 물을 때는 Doe Paul ~?이 아니라 Is Paul ~?로 물어야 한다.
3. No, they aren't.
   they 다음에는 isn't가 아니라 aren't가 와야 한다.
4. No, I do not(don't).
   Do you ~로 물으면 대답은 Yes/No 다음에 I 혹은 we로 대답이 가능한데, 사진에 1명이 등장하므로 I로 대답한다.

통합서술형

1. Is, it, isn't
2. Are, you, I, am, Are, you, No, am, not
3. Do, you, I, do, do, you, No, I, don't

해석 | Kate: 당신 이름이 Jack인가요?
Bill: 아뇨, 그렇지 않아요. 내 이름은 Bill이에요.
Kate: 13살인가요?
Bill: 네, 그래요.
Kate: Jack, 당신은 어때요? 당신도 13살인가요?
Jack: 아뇨, 그렇지 않아요. 저는 14살이에요.
Kate: 마이애미에 사나요?
Jack: 네, 그래요. 그래서 서핑을 좋아해요.
Kate: Bill, 당신도 서핑을 좋아하나요?
Bill: 아뇨, 그렇지 않아요. 나는 농구를 좋아해요.

CHAPTER 02 과거시제

CORE 04 과거시제

Grammar Check p.18

1. was	2. were	3. Was
4. visited	5. did	6. came

01 p.19

1. She was my English teacher.

2. We were interested in the news.
3. The history class was not boring.
4. Were Kate and Jane your friends?
5. Were you at the library?

02

1. He planned
2. I didn't wash
3. They studied the disease
4. Did the door close
5. She bought the gift
6. Jonathan had breakfast
7. We made dolls

03 p.20

1. went shopping
2. did not(didn't) play basketball with his friends
3. sent an e-mail to Mary
4. did not(didn't) clean his room
5. made sandwiches for his family

통합서술형

gave, played, played, did not(didn't) play, sang, was, had

해석 | 어제 나는 나의 음악 동아리 회원들과 병원에 갔다. 우리는 어린이 환자들에게 음악회를 열어주었다. Tom은 기타를 연주했고 Edward는 드럼을 연주했다. 나는 아무것도 연주하지 않았다. 나는 노래를 불렀다. 아주 흥미진진한 음악회였다. 모두가 재미있는 시간을 가졌다.

CORE 05 미래시제

Grammar Check p.21

1. will, know
2. am, going, to, take
3. will, not, fall
4. Will, come
5. is, not, going, to, open

01 p.22

1. I will(am going to) be a nurse.
2. We will not(won't/are not going to) write a letter to Bill.
3. Will you(Are you going to) clean the windows?
4. The class is not(isn't) going to start soon.
5. Is Robin's brother going to leave for London this evening?

02

1. is not going to play computer games
2. will be 14 years old next year
   is going to study hard
   is not going to be late for school
3. Dad will be 40 years old next year.
   He is not going to eat hamburgers.
   He is going to be kind to his neighbors.

03 p.23

1. I am going to jog
2. Ted will visit the house
3. The train is not going to leave
4. Will he study history
5. Allan and Ed are going to finish the work
6. Will she help her mom

통합서술형

(1) will(is going to) make a speech
(2) will(is going to) play music
(3) will(are going to) have lunch
(4) will(is going to) play *Snow White*
(5) will(are going to) hold a dance party

해석 | Rainbow 학교에서는 5월 7일 축제를 개최합니다. Smith 씨께서 10시 30분에 연설을 하실 예정입니다. 연설이 끝나면 학교 밴드가 음악을 연주할 것입니다. 12시 30분에 점심을 먹을 겁니다. 점심 식사 후, 드라마 동아리가 *백설공주*를 상연할 예정입니다. 4시 30분에 댄스파티를 열 것입니다. Rainbow 학교 축제에 오시지 않으시겠습니까?

CORE 06 진행시제

Grammar Check p.24

1. I am reading a novel.
2. He was cooking in the kitchen.
3. They were not(weren't) learning Japanese then.
4. Were you cleaning your room at that time?

Check

1. coming 2. having 3. running 4. tying

01 p.25

1. is, riding
2. am, not, talking
3. Are, sitting
4. was, tying
5. Were, moving
6. were, not, swimming

02

1. She is making pasta now.
   현재진행형은 「be동사+동사-ing」로 나타낸다.
2. Sam is not going to the market.
   진행형의 부정은 be동사 뒤에 not을 쓴다.
3. Was he using a fax at that time?
   주어가 3인칭 단수이므로 was가 알맞다.
4. He and I were solving math problems.
   주어가 '그와 나' 복수이므로 were가 알맞다.
5. Are you lying on the sofa now?
   현재진행형: be동사+동사-ing
6. You and your sister were shopping at the mall.
   주어가 '너와 너의 여동생' 복수이므로 were가 알맞다.

03 p.26

1. He is shopping now.
2. Were you writing a letter?
3. Tom and Amy are running outdoors.
4. The cat was not(wasn't) lying on the sofa.

통합서술형

is jumping, is jogging, is singing, is playing, is riding, am lying, are having

해석 | 나와 내 친구들은 지금 공원에 있다. Sue는 줄넘기를 하고 있고, Bill은 아빠와 조깅을 하고 있다. Ann은 노래를 부르고 있고, Bob은 기타를 치고 있다. Cathy는 자전거를 타고 있고, 나는 잔디 위에 누워 있다. 우리는 공원에서 즐거운 시간을 보내고 있다!

CHAPTER 03 조동사

CORE 07 can / may

Grammar Check p.28

1. A giraffe can run very fast.
   조동사 뒤에는 동사원형이 온다.
2. The work may be very difficult for you.
   may는 주어에 따라 형태가 변하지 않는다.
3. The team cannot(can't) play tomorrow.
   can의 부정형은 cannot(can't)이다.
4. Are you able to move this furniture?
   be able to에서 to가 빠졌으므로 넣어야 한다.
5. May I ask a question?
   may의 의문문: May+주어+동사원형?
6. They may not be at home at this time.
   부정어는 조동사 바로 뒤에 온다.

01 p.29

1. can
2. may
3. Can
4. May(Can)
5. is, able, to
6. may(can)

02

1. She may win
2. We cannot(can't) find
3. The baby is able to stand up
4. You can(may) invite Evan

5. Can you wait for him
6. May(Can) I see
7. Sally and Tim may not meet

03 p.30

1. Can you open the window?
2. She can(is able to) repair the car.
3. May(can) I dance with you?
4. You cannot(can't) read aloud here.

통합서술형

(1) can play, can't(cannot) play
(2) can eat, can't(cannot) eat
(3) can ride, can't(cannot) ride

해석 | 나는 세 명의 좋은 친구들이 있다. David는 스페인어를 말할 수 있지만 Paul은 스페인어를 말하지 못한다. Sara는 피아노를 칠 수 있지만 David는 피아노를 치지 못한다. Paul은 젓가락으로 먹을 수 있지만 Sara는 젓가락으로 먹지 못한다. David는 스케이트보드를 탈 수 있지만 Paul은 스케이트보드를 타지 못한다.

CORE 08 must / should

Grammar Check p.31

1. have, to
2. ought, to
3. Do, have, to
4. should, not
5. don't, have, to

01 p.32

1. He ought to make dinner today.
   ought to에서 to가 빠졌으므로 넣어야 한다.
2. My brother has to prepare for the exam.
   have to는 주어와 시제에 따라 형태가 변한다. 주어가 3인칭 단수이므로 has가 되어야 한다.
3. We must not break the law.
   must의 부정형은 must not이다.
4. Should she answer the question?
   should의 의문문: Should+주어+동사원형?
5. You don't have to get up early tomorrow.
   have to의 부정형은 don't have to이다.
6. Does Jessica have to wear glasses?
   have to의 의문문에 쓰인 do도 주어와 시제에 따라 형태가 변한다.

02

1. Students must not(mustn't) leave
2. You ought to come
3. He must be surprised
4. Does Sally have to bring
5. She must be a doctor
6. Steve doesn't have(need) to mow

03 p.33

1. Should we paint this wall?
2. She must be a math teacher.
3. We should not(shouldn't) waste food.
4. Ann doesn't have(need) to take the medicine.

통합서술형

1. must fasten
2. must not(mustn't) take
3. must wear
4. must not(mustn't) swim

해석 | 직원들은 손을 씻어야 합니다.
이곳에서 담배를 피우면 안 됩니다.
승객들은 안전벨트를 매야 합니다.
방문객들은 이곳에서 사진을 찍으면 안 됩니다.
사람들은 구명조끼를 착용해야 합니다.
이 강에서 수영하면 안 됩니다.

CHAPTER 04 명사와 대명사

CORE 09 셀 수 있는 명사와 셀 수 없는 명사 / There is(are)

Grammar Check p. 36

1. elephants
2. buildings
3. salt
4. a car
5. advice
6. Jane

Check

1. teeth
2. fish
3. women

01 p.37

1. dishes
2. babies
3. men
4. buses
5. potatoes
6. leaves
7. feet
8. benches
9. knives
10. geese

02

1. My sister has red hair.
   hair는 셀 수 없는 명사로 항상 단수형으로 쓴다.
2. We ate bread for lunch.
   bread는 셀 수 없는 명사로 항상 단수형으로 쓴다.
3. Ashley teaches children at a preschool.
   child의 복수형은 children이다.
4. There are some books on the desk.
   some books가 복수이므로 there 다음에 are를 쓴다.
5. Jason finished five stories.
   5편의 이야기들이므로 복수형인 stories를 쓴다.
6. She put some money into her account.
   money는 셀 수 없는 명사로 항상 단수형으로 쓴다.
7. He told us his opinion on life.
   life는 셀 수 없는 명사로 앞에 a를 붙일 수 없다.

03 p.38

1. There are four children
2. There is a bench
3. leaves and flowers
4. sandwiches and juice

통합서술형

prepare knives, will buy bread, will bring potatoes

CORE 10 셀 수 없는 명사의 수량 표현

Grammar Check p. 39

1. two cups of coffee
2. two bowls of salad
3. three glasses of beer
4. two bottles of water
5. four pairs of socks
6. four pieces of furniture
7. three pieces of paper
8. two loaves of bread

01 p.40

1. a pair of glasses
2. a cup of tea
3. two pieces of cake
4. two bowls of soup
5. three loaves of bread
6. four glasses of juice
7. a piece of information

02

1. Lena made ten cups of coffee.
   앞에 ten이 있으므로 복수형인 cups를 쓴다.
2. My sister exchanged six pairs of jeans.
   앞에 six가 있으므로 복수형인 pairs를 쓴다.

3. Julia received two bottles of perfume.
perfume은 셀 수 없는 명사로 복수형은 bottles of perfume으로 나타낸다.

4. They bought five slices of pizza.
pizza는 slice로 세며 복수형은 pizzas가 아닌 slices로 쓴다.

5. I gave four bars of soap to Alicia.
soap은 셀 수 없는 명사로 단수형으로만 써야 한다.

6. The boy ate three bowls of rice.
rice는 셀 수 없는 명사로 단수형으로만 써야 한다.

03 p.41

(1) Dad bought a pair of jeans.
(2) Mom bought three pieces of furniture.
(3) Susie ate two bowls of salad.
(4) Susie's brother bought five bars of soap.

통합서술형

1. two glasses of juice, a piece(slice) of cake
2. two loaves of bread, a bottle of water, a bowl of soup

해석 | 1. Paul은 피자 두 조각을 주문했다. 그는 주스 두 잔을 마셨다. 그는 케이크 한 조각을 즐겼다.
2. Minsu는 빵 두 덩어리를 먹었다. 그는 물 한 잔을 마셨다. 그는 수프 한 그릇을 먹었다.

CORE 11 지시대명사 / 비인칭 주어 it

Grammar Check p. 42

1. it	2. this
3. that	4. These
5. It	6. Those

01 p.43

1. I have a doll. It is pretty.
앞에 언급된 명사는 it으로 나타낸다.

2. Are those your classmates?
classmates가 복수이므로 those를 쓴다.

3. It snows a lot in winter.
날씨를 나타내므로 비인칭 주어인 it을 쓴다.

4. These leather shoes are very expensive.
shoes가 복수이므로 These를 쓴다.

5. Is this James' sister in the picture?
James' sister는 단수이므로 this로 쓴다.

6. It is 2 kilometers from the station to the hospital.
거리를 나타내므로 비인칭 주어인 it을 쓴다.

02

1. It is spring
2. These are my teachers
3. it is blue
4. Is it cold and windy
5. It is 3 kilometers
6. These are my pencils, those are your pens

03 p.44

It was Sunday, It was warm and sunny,
This is my aunt, Those are my cousins

통합서술형

It is May 6(th)., It is 9 o'clock., this, those

해석 | Mina: 오늘은 며칠이니?
Jinsu: 5월 6일이야.
Mina: 지금은 몇 시니?
Jinsu: 9시야.
Mina: 탁자 위에 있는 이것은 무엇이니?
Jinsu: 그것은 꽃병이야.
Mina: 소파 위에 있는 저것들은 무엇이니?
Jinsu: 그것들은 로봇들이야.

CORE 12 재귀대명사

Grammar Check p. 45

1. myself	2. himself
3. herself	4. themselves
5. yourself	

Check

1. for oneself 2. of oneself 3. enjoy oneself

01 p.46

1. I myself made the travel plans.
   '직접'이라는 의미로 주어를 강조하는 강조용법의 재귀대명사인 myself가 알맞다.
2. The window closed of itself.
   of oneself: 저절로
3. They enjoyed themselves in the pool.
   they의 재귀대명사는 themselves이다.
4. Did he finish the essay himself?
   '직접'이라는 의미이므로 재귀대명사 himself를 쓴다.
5. The woman lives by herself in the city.
   by oneself: 혼자
6. My father and I painted the wall ourselves.
   we의 재귀대명사는 ourselves이다.

02

1. protect themselves
2. a letter to myself
3. Help yourself to
4. the bookstore by(for) yourself
5. themselves moved the boxes(moved the boxes themselves)
6. himself sold a pair of boots(sold a pair of boots himself)

03 p.47

1. The door opened of itself.
2. People enjoy themselves at the park.
3. He runs by himself.
4. Help yourself to cookies.

통합서술형

1. Mom and I cooked chicken and salad ourselves.
   주어가 엄마와 나이므로 ourselves가 알맞다.
2. My brother made lemonade by(for) himself.
   '혼자' 혹은 '혼자 힘으로'라는 뜻의 by(for) himself가 알맞다.
3. My grandparents helped themselves to the dishes.
   help oneself to: 마음껏 먹다
4. We enjoyed ourselves at dinner.
   we의 재귀대명사는 ourselves이다.

해석 | 엄마는 지난 주 토요일에 조부모님을 집에 초대하셨다. 엄마와 나는 닭고기와 샐러드를 직접 요리했다. 남동생은 혼자 레몬에이드를 만들었다. 조부모님은 음식들을 마음껏 드셨다. 우리는 저녁 식사를 즐겼다.

CORE 13 부정대명사

Grammar Check p. 48

1. one 2. another
3. others 4. the others

Check

1. One, the other 2. Some

01 p.49

1. another 2. the others
3. One, the others 4. Some, others
5. One, another, the other 6. ones

02

1. This ring is big. Do you have a smaller one?
   앞에 나온 셀 수 있는 명사를 대신할 때는 one을 쓴다.
2. I have two balls. One is blue, and the other is red.
   '(둘 중) 나머지 하나'를 의미할 때는 the other을 쓴다.
3. We should try to be helpful to others.
   '다른 사람들'을 의미할 때는 others를 쓴다.
4. Some like mountains, and others like rivers.
   '(여럿 중) 또 다른 일부'를 의미할 때는 others를 쓴다.

5. The shoes are large. I'll try smaller ones.
앞에 나온 셀 수 있는 명사의 복수형은 ones로 받는다.

6. She has three presents. One is for Bob, another is for Jin, and the other is for Tim.
'(셋 중) 나머지 하나'를 가리킬 때는 the other를 쓴다.

03 p.50

1. One is a book, and the other is an album.
2. Some like music, and the others like art.
3. One is a chair, another is a desk, and the other is a table.
4. Some drank coffee, and others drank tea.
5. One is a car, and the others are buses.

통합서술형

1. the others are boys
2. One is an apple, another is an orange, and the other is a banana.
3. One is a dog, and the other is a cat.

해석 | 1. Jina는 친구들이 있다. 한 명은 소녀이고, 나머지 전부는 소년들이다.
2. 탁자 위에 과일이 세 개 있다. 하나는 사과이고, 또 다른 하나는 오렌지이고, 나머지 하나는 바나나이다.
3. Tim은 애완동물 두 마리가 있다. 한 마리는 개이고, 나머지 한 마리는 고양이이다.

CHAPTER 05 형용사와 부사

CORE 14 형용사와 부사

Grammar Check p.52

1. The bird has colorful feathers
2. The book seems interesting
3. He saw someone famous
4. She always studies

Check

1. beautifully
2. heavily
3. comfortably

01 p.53

1. Your voice sounds strange to me.
주어를 설명하는 주격보어로 형용사인 strange를 써야 한다.

2. She can't eat anything cold.
-thing으로 끝나는 부정대명사는 형용사가 뒤에서 수식한다.

3. The student is often late for school.
빈도부사는 be동사 뒤에 온다.

4. The young students are really smart.
주어를 설명하는 주격보어로 형용사인 smart가 와야 한다.

5. Surprisingly, he passed the exam.
문장 전체를 수식할 수 있는 것은 부사이다.

6. William will never know the secret.
빈도부사는 조동사 뒤, 일반동사 앞에 온다.

02

1. greets me happily
2. practices hard
3. is nearly
4. This blouse matches perfectly
5. He hardly drives
6. I will work late

03 p.54

works hard, is a great chef, makes something delicious, is surprisingly messy, hardly cleans

통합서술형

1. always plays
2. usually reads
3. often rides
4. sometimes volunteers
5. never plays

해석 | Ben은 항상 피아노를 친다. 그는 대개 책을 읽는다. 그는 종종 자전거를 탄다. 그는 가끔 도서관에서 봉사를 한다. 그는 컴퓨터 게임을 절대 하지 않는다.

CORE 15 수량 형용사

Grammar Check p.55

1. many
2. A few
3. few
4. a little
5. much
6. little
7. any

01 p.56

1. some
2. any
3. many
4. a few
5. much
6. a little
7. Few
8. much
9. any
10. little

02

1. Many foreigners visited the place today.
   many+셀 수 있는 명사: 많은
2. Janet didn't buy any bread at the bakery.
   부정문에서는 any가 쓰인다.
3. He put a little salt into the soup.
   a little+셀 수 없는 명사: 조금 있는
4. The child spilled much juice on the table.
   much+셀 수 없는 명사: 많은
5. The painter sold few paintings in his lifetime.
   few+셀 수 있는 명사: 거의 없는
6. I have no fruit, but she has some bananas.
   긍정문에서는 some이 쓰인다.

03 p.57

(1) Jane ate a few(some) hot dogs.
(2) I ate few hot dogs.
(3) Paul drank a little(some) milk.
(4) Jane drank little milk.
(5) I drank much milk.

통합서술형

1. much
2. a little bread
3. a few
4. any sandwiches
5. some

해석 | Sara는 많은 빵을 샀다. 그러나 Jack은 조금의 빵만 샀다. 그녀는 또한 야채도 샀다. 그녀는 조금의 샌드위치를 만들었다. 그러나 그는 약간의 샌드위치도 만들지 않았다. 그녀는 그에게 말했다. "샌드위치를 좀 먹을래?"

CHAPTER 06 비교

CORE 16 형용사·부사의 비교급과 최상급

Grammar Check p.60

1. smaller
2. coldest
3. more, popular
4. dirtier
5. most, confidently

Check

1. better, best
2. less, least
3. more, most
4. worse, worst
5. later, latest

01 p.61

1. warmer than
2. the cutest
3. the busiest
4. the biggest
5. better than
6. the latest
7. worse than

02

1. She is younger than my sister.
   than 앞에는 비교급이 온다.
2. Her idea is the most creative in our company.
   최상급 앞에는 the가 온다.

3. This bed is the most comfortable.
3음절 이상인 단어의 최상급은 「most+원급」이다.

4. Jane fixed the problem more carefully than you.
3음절 이상인 단어의 비교급은 「more+원급」이다.

5. David's book is more interesting than that book.
than 앞에는 비교급이 온다.

6. Walter is the oldest player on the team.
old는 -est를 붙여서 최상급을 만든다.

03 p.62

1. more expensive than, the narrowest
2. the cheapest
3. wider than, the most expensive

통합서술형

1. is bigger than, is the biggest, is smaller than, is the smallest,
2. are younger than, is the oldest

해석 | Max는 크다. Max는 Vino와 Bota보다 더 크다. Max는 셋 중에서 가장 크다. Vino는 작다. Vino는 Bota보다 더 작다. Vino는 셋 중에서 가장 작다.
Vino와 Max는 여섯 살이다. 그들은 Bota보다 더 어리다. Bota는 셋 중에서 가장 나이가 많다.

CORE 17 비교급·최상급의 주요 표현

Grammar Check p.63

1. less popular than his brother
2. is the least lazy
3. The more, the fatter
4. one of the safest places
5. getting thinner and thinner
6. the fifth thickest book

01 p.64

1. His health is getting better and better.
비교급+and+비교급: 점점 더 ~한

2. It is less warm today than yesterday.
「less+형용사·부사+than」 표현이므로 less 뒤에 형용사의 원급인 warm이 와야 한다.

3. He has the fourth strongest arm of the students.
the+서수+최상급: …번 째로 가장 ~한

4. Saturn is one of the largest planets in the solar system.
one of the+최상급+복수 명사: 가장 ~한 …중 하나

5. The higher we went up, the colder we felt.
the+비교급, the+비교급: 더 ~할수록 더 …한(하게)

6. The moment was the least happy of my life.
「the least+형용사·부사」 표현이므로 the least 뒤에 형용사의 원급인 happy가 와야 한다.

02

1. less cheap than
2. hotter and hotter
3. one of the largest deserts
4. the least difficult
5. is the third most intelligent
6. The older, the higher

03 p.65

the second youngest
The more, the higher he jumps
he is getting faster and faster
He is one of the best players on the team.

통합서술형

1. less, than, tallest, the least tall
2. less heavy than, the second heaviest, the least heavy

해석 | Andy는 모두 중에서 키가 가장 크다. Tina는 Andy보다 키가 덜 크다. Joel은 모두 중에서 키가 세 번째로 가장 크다. Becky는 모두 중에서 키가 가장 덜 크다.
Tina는 모두 중에서 가장 무겁다. Joel은 Tina보다 덜 무겁다. Andy는 모두 중에서 두 번째로 가장 무겁다. Becky는 모두 중에서 가장 덜 무겁다.

CORE 18 원급의 주요 표현

Grammar Check p.66

1. as difficult as English
2. not as smart as her sister
3. as quietly as I could
4. as fast as me
5. as slowly as possible
6. not so busy as a week ago
7. as much as he can
8. as carefully as I did

01 p.67

1. as tall as
2. not as(so) spicy as
3. as early as possible(I can)
4. as attractive as
5. as politely as possible(she could)
6. not live as(so) long as

02

1. Philosophy is as important as science.
   as+원급+as: …만큼 ~한
2. I will call you back as quickly as I can.
   as+원급+as+주어+can: 가능한 한 ~하게
3. Sharks are not as big as whales.
   「not as(so)+원급+as」 표현이므로 not as 순서가 되어야 한다.
4. These peaches are as sweet as honey.
   「as+원급+as」 표현이므로 so는 as가 되어야 한다.
5. She solved the problem as soon as possible.
   「as+원급+as possible」 표현이므로 원급인 soon이 와야 한다.
6. My sister does not work as actively as my brother.
   「as+원급+as」 표현이므로 so는 as가 되어야 한다.

03 p.68

Barbie is as cute as Minky.
Barbie is not as(so) fast as Minky
we play with them as much as possible(we can)

통합서술형

1. is as heavy as, is not as(so) wide as
2. is as expensive as, is not as(so) high as

해석 | A 탁자는 B 탁자만큼 무겁다. A 탁자는 B 탁자만큼 넓지 않다. B 탁자는 A 탁자만큼 비싸다. B 탁자는 A 탁자만큼 높지 않다.

CHAPTER 07 문장의 종류

CORE 19 의문사가 있는 의문문

Grammar Check p.70

1. Who 2. What 3. Where
4. When 5. How 6. Why

Check

1. old 2. far 3. many

01 p.71

1. Where is the post office?
2. Who is the man over there?
3. When did the musical end?
4. What is your favorite color?
5. Why do people hate the comedian?
6. How often does he go to the movies?

02

1. How old is the dog?
2. When does the concert start?
3. Where does your grandfather live?
4. What did they eat for lunch?
5. Who is your favorite singer?
6. How many countries did you visit?

03 p.72

1. Where are you from?
   where: 어디에 / when: 언제
2. What is her name?
   what: 무엇 / how: 어떻게
3. How old is your brother?
   오래된 정도를 물을 때는 how old를 쓴다.
4. Why are you so happy?
   why: 왜 / what: 무엇
5. When did you buy the bike?
   when: 언제 / where: 어디에

통합서술형

Maureen, Where, are, you, Canada, How, old, are, How, many, What, play, the, violin

해석 | George: 이름이 무엇이니?

Maureen: 내 이름은 Maureen이야.

George: 어디서 왔니?

Maureen: 난 캐나다에서 왔어.

George: 몇 살이니?

Maureen: 14살이야.

George: 가족은 총 몇 명이야?

Maureen: 5명이야.

George: 여가 시간에는 무엇을 하니?

Maureen: 난 바이올린을 켜.

CORE 20 명령문 / 권유문 / 감탄문

Grammar Check p.73

1. Clean your room.
2. Don't(Never) walk on the grass.
3. Let's go for a swim.
4. Let's not close the windows.
5. How delicious this cake is!
6. What a huge dog (it is)!

01 p.74

1. Be kind to your neighbors.
   형용사의 명령형은 형용사 앞에 Be동사를 쓰면 된다.
2. Let's go hiking on Sunday.
   권유문: Let's+동사원형
3. Don't(Never) eat junk food.
   부정 명령문: Don't(Never)+동사원형
4. Let's not play computer games.
   부정 권유문: Let's not+동사원형
5. What an exciting story it is!
   what 감탄문: What a/an+형용사+명사(+주어+동사)!
6. How beautifully Jasmine sings!
   how 감탄문: How+형용사/부사(+주어+동사)!

02

1. What a nice gift (it is)!
2. What smart students (they are)!
3. How cute the baby is!
4. How beautiful the houses are!
5. What a big numbrella you have!
6. How fast the car goes!

03 p.75

1. Don't be late
2. Let's play basketball
3. Never open
4. Let's not talk loudly
5. Please wash your hands

통합서술형

What, How, Turn off, Don't touch, Don't take

해석 | 알립니다

Great Art Gallery에 오신 것을 환영합니다.

저희 갤러리는 정말 훌륭한 그림들을 보유하고 있습니다! 그 그림들은 얼마나 아름다운지! 조용히 해주시고 다음의 규칙들을 지켜 주십시오.

1. 갤러리에서는 휴대전화를 끄세요.
2. 그림에 손대지 마세요.
3. 사진을 찍지 마세요.

CORE 21 부가의문문 / 선택의문문

Grammar Check p. 76

1. aren't, you
2. does, he
3. will, you
4. shall, we
5. or
6. Who, or

01 p.77

1. It is a nice day, isn't it?
2. Computers work fast, don't they?
3. You can't play the violin, can you?
4. You and Tom aren't in the same class, are you?
5. Be a good boy, will you?
6. Let's go to the movies, shall we?

02

1. She is your English teacher, isn't she?
   부가의문문의 부정형 동사는 반드시 축약형을 쓴다.
2. Calvin can drive a car, can't he?
   부가의문문의 주어는 반드시 인칭대명사를 사용한다.
3. Let's join our school band, shall we?
   Let's 명령문의 부가의문문은 shall we?이다.
4. Don't be noisy in the library, will you?
   명령문의 부가의문문은 will you?이다.
5. How do you go there, by bus or by train?
   선택의문문의 접속사는 or이다.
6. Allan wasn't in Paris last week, was he?
   be동사의 부가의문문은 be동사로 쓴다.

03 p.78

1. You can't swim, can you?
2. The Eiffel Tower is in France, isn't it?
3. Is she reading a book or a letter?
4. Let's move this desk, shall we?
5. Which does he like better, pizza or pasta?
6. Buy milk on your way home, will you?

통합서술형

will, you, shall, we, which, or, spaghetti, steak, will, you, juice

해석 | Jane: Mike, 나에게 메뉴판을 건네줘, 알았지?
Mike: 여기 있어.
Jane: 옥수수 수프를 먹자, 그럴 거지?
Mike: 좋아. 그러면 넌 스테이크와 스파게티 중 어느 것을 더 좋아해?
Jane: 나는 스파게티를 더 좋아해. 너는 어때?
Mike: 나는 스테이크를 원해. 또 커피도 좀 마시고 싶어.
Jane: 넌 이미 커피를 두 잔 마셨어. 더 이상 커피 마시지 마, 알았지?
Mike: 그러면 주스를 마실게.

CHAPTER 08 to부정사

CORE 22 명사적 용법

Grammar Check p. 80

1. 주어
2. 목적어
3. 주어
4. 보어
5. 목적어
6. 보어
7. 목적어

Check

1. to talk
2. to learn
3. to win

01 p.81

1. To make a plan is
2. loves to eat French food
3. is to travel the world
4. is interesting to make foreign friends
5. planned to visit the museum
6. is to grow apple trees

02

1. To learn taekwondo is very exciting.
   동사 learn을 주어로 쓸 때는 To learn으로 쓴다.

2. It is fun to run on the beach.
「It(가주어) ~ to부정사(진주어) ...」 구문이므로 to run으로 쓴다.

3. Jenny likes to draw pictures.
동사 like는 to부정사를 목적어로 취하므로 to draw를 쓴다.

4. Eric's hope is to become a singer.
동사 become을 보어로 쓸 때는 to become으로 쓴다.

5. They expected to see her again.
동사 expect는 to부정사를 목적어로 취하므로 to see를 쓴다.

6. It is impossible to finish the work in a week.
「It(가주어) ~ to부정사(진주어) ...」 구문이므로 It ~ to finish로 쓴다.

03 p.82

1. To play baseball is
2. started to clean the house
3. is to ride a bike
4. It is not easy to lose
5. failed to make a reservation
6. is to finish school next year
7. To write in a diary every day is

통합서술형

1. to cook food, To watch food shows, to become a cook
2. to go to the mountains, to take pictures, to exhibit flower photos

해석 | 나는 두 명의 친구 Jack과 Mina가 있다. Jack은 주말에 요리하는 것을 좋아한다. 또한 텔레비전에서 요리쇼를 보는 것도 그가 좋아하는 것이다. 그의 희망은 요리사가 되는 것이다. Mina는 아빠와 함께 산에 가는 것을 좋아한다. 그녀는 "꽃 사진들을 찍는 것은 신나."라고 말한다. 그녀의 꿈은 꽃 사진들을 전시하는 것이다.

CORE 23 형용사적 용법

Grammar Check p. 83

1. many books to read
2. time to take a break
3. a colored pencil to write with
4. funny stories to tell you
5. someone to help her
6. an apartment to live in
7. anything special to do this weekend

01 p.84

1. a train to catch
2. anybody to play with
3. money to buy toys
4. a hotel to stay at
5. no time to go to the supermarket
6. a partner to dance with
7. anything important to remember

02

1. Susan has a lot of heavy boxes to move.
동사 move가 명사를 수식하려면 to move로 써야 한다.

2. Please give me something to read.
to부정사가 형용사처럼 대명사를 수식하려면 뒤에서 수식해야 한다.

3. Her grandparents built a new house to live in.
집 안에서 사는 것이므로 전치사 in을 써야 한다.

4. Does Jimmy want anything sweet to eat?
-thing으로 끝나는 대명사는 형용사가 뒤에서 수식한다.

5. I am looking for friends to play with.
함께 놀 친구들이므로 전치사 with를 써야 한다.

6. The children needed paper to write on.
종이 위에 쓰는 것이므로 전치사 on을 써야 한다.

03 p.85

(1) a book to read
(2) something sweet to eat
(3) a puppy to play with

통합서술형

vegetables to make salad
something cold to drink
birthday cards to write on
pretty paper to decorate with

해석 | 내일 Hana의 친구들은 그녀를 위해서 깜짝 파티를 열 것이다. Eddy는 샐러드를 만들 채소를 가져올 것이다. Jumi는 차가운 마실 것을 준비할 것이다. Gabriel은 쓸 생일 카드를 만들 것이다. Tommy는 장식할 예쁜 종이를 살 것이다.

CORE 24 부사적 용법

Grammar Check p. 86

1. to buy
2. to fail
3. to find
4. to solve
5. to watch
6. to fight

01 p.87

1. 그 여자는 체중을 줄이기 위해서 운동한다.
2. 나는 그를 만나서 놀랐다.
3. 그 소년은 자라서 선생님이 되었다.
4. 이 책은 이해하기 어렵다.
5. 그들은 팬더를 보기 위해서 동물원에 갔다.
6. 나의 할머니는 90세까지 사셨다.

02

1. worked hard to succeed
2. is deep to measure
3. was glad to receive his letter
4. grew up to become a guitarist
5. went to the kitchen to make dinner
6. awoke up to find herself alone in the house
7. was pleased to spend time with his cousins

03 p.88

1. to make new things, to become an inventor, to invent light bulbs
2. to study physics, to become a scientist, to find new materials

통합서술형

(1) I practiced hard to win the contest.
문장의 의미상 to부정사가 와서 '~하기 위해서'라는 목적을 나타내야 한다.

(2) The contest was difficult to win.
형용사 다음에 to부정사가 와서 '~하기에'라는 의미의 정도를 나타내야 한다.

(3) I was disappointed to lose the contest.
감정 형용사 disappointed 다음에 to부정사가 오면 감정의 원인을 나타낸다.

(4) I will grow up to become a famous singer.
grow up 다음에 to부정사가 오면 결과를 나타낸다.

해석 | 나의 꿈은 가수가 되는 것이다. 그래서 나는 노래 대회에 참가하기로 결심했다. 나는 대회에서 우승하기 위해서 열심히 연습했다. 그 대회는 우승하기에 어려웠다. 나는 대회에서 져서 실망했다. 하지만 나는 절대 나의 꿈을 포기하지 않을 것이다. 나는 자라서 유명한 가수가 될 것이다.

CHAPTER 09 동명사

CORE 25 동명사의 역할

Grammar Check p. 90

1. 주어
2. 동사의 목적어
3. 보어
4. 전치사의 목적어
5. 주어

Check

1. 동명사
2. 현재분사
3. 현재분사
4. 동명사

01 p.91

1. Studying biology is
2. enjoys eating Thai food
3. is playing golf
4. Keeping your promises is
5. was proud of passing the exam
6. is climbing the Alps this summer

02

1. Playing(To play) basketball with friends is fun.
   동사 play를 주어로 쓸 때는 to부정사 또는 동명사로 쓴다.
2. Does Emma enjoy growing plants and flowers?
   동사 enjoy는 동명사를 목적어로 취한다.
3. The girl's habit is biting(to bite) her nails.
   동사 bite를 보어로 쓸 때는 to부정사 또는 동명사로 쓴다.
4. I am afraid of riding a bike.
   전치사 of 다음에는 동명사를 쓴다.
5. He practiced driving a car.
   동사 practice는 동명사를 목적어로 취한다.
6. They are not excited about watching a movie.
   전치사 about 다음에는 동명사를 쓴다.

03 p.92

1. is interested in writing novels
2. consider forming a tennis club
3. Taking(To take) the subway is faster
4. is designing(to design) women's clothes
5. is fond of baking cookies
6. Looking(To look) at the stars at night is
7. avoids using his cell phone on the bus

통합서술형

1. eating bamboo leaves, climbing trees, resting(to rest) during the day
2. eating(to eat) leaves and fruit, catching things with their nose, Taking(To take) a mud shower

해석 | 팬더는 숲에서 대나무 잎사귀들을 먹는 것을 즐긴다. 그들은 나무를 오르는 것에 능숙하다. 그들의 습성은 낮 동안 쉬는 것이다. 코끼리는 나뭇잎들과 과일 먹는 것을 좋아한다. 그들은 코로 물건을 잡는 것에 능숙하다. 진흙 샤워를 하는 것이 그들의 습성이다.

CORE 26 동명사·to부정사를 목적어로 취하는 동사

Grammar Check p. 93

1. singing
2. drawing(to draw)
3. to receive
4. practicing(to practice)
5. closing
6. to build

01 p.94

1. I finished answering all his questions.
   동사 finish는 동명사를 목적어로 취한다.
2. The actor hoped to receive the award.
   동사 hope는 to부정사를 목적어로 취한다.
3. The boys started watching(to watch) the soccer game.
   동사 start는 to부정사와 동명사 둘 다 목적어로 취할 수 있다.
4. Will the company keep producing computers?
   동사 keep은 동명사를 목적어로 취한다.
5. My brother promised to go to the dentist.
   동사 promise는 to부정사를 목적어로 취한다.

02

1. remember locking the door
2. remember to post the package
3. tried to solve the problem
4. tried making kites
5. Don't forget to return
6. forget seeing Emily
7. stopped to talk with me
8. stopped reading the newspaper

03 p.95

walking, seeing, to visit, to answer

통합서술형

drinking(to drink) coffee, to take pictures, to speak French, walking along the streets

해석 | Tina의 가족은 지난 여름 파리에 갔다. 엄마는 카페에서 커피 마시는 것을 좋아하셨다. 아빠는 그 도시의 사진을 찍기로 계획하셨다. Tina는 걷다가 사람들과 프랑스어를 하기 위해서 발걸음을 멈추었다. Tina의 남동생은 계속 길을 따라 걸었다.

CHAPTER 10 전치사와 접속사

CORE 27 전치사

Grammar Check p. 98

1. at 2. during 3. on
4. in 5. in front of

Check

1. out of 2. for 3. across

01 p.99

1. in 2. on 3. after
4. before 5. at, in 6. on

02

1. behind the building
2. for one hour
3. along the railroad tracks
4. over the mountain
5. until ten o'clock
6. up the stairs, down the stairs

03 p.100

1. There is a family picture on the wall.
   벽과 같이 표면에 접촉한 상태에는 전치사 on을 쓴다.
2. Kelly studied for her test for three hours.
   숫자로 표현되는 기간에는 전치사 for를 쓴다.
3. The swimming pool is in front of the hotel.
   in front of: ~ 앞에
4. I have breakfast at 7 o'clock in the morning.
   시각에는 전치사 at을 쓴다. 하루의 때에는 전치사 in을 쓴다.
5. Laura lived in France in 2008.
   국가와 같은 넓은 장소와 연도에는 전치사 in을 쓴다.
6. Paul will leave for New York on September 26th.
   for: ~을 향하여. 월 앞에는 전치사 in을 쓰지만, 날짜가 왔으므로 전치사 on을 쓴다.

통합서술형

in, along, over, under, on, in front of

해석 | 오후에 공원에는 사람들이 많이 있다. 몇몇 사람들은 길을 따라 조깅을 하고 있다. 새들은 나무 위를 날고 있고, 아이들은 나무 밑에서 놀고 있다. 두 사람은 나무 앞에 있는 벤치 위에 앉아 있다.

CORE 28 등위접속사

Grammar Check p. 101

1. and 2. but 3. or
4. so 5. or

Check

1. or 2. and 3. and 4. or

01 p.102

1. but 2. and 3. so
4. or 5. and 6. or

02

1. a pencil and a notebook
2. cold but tasty
3. so we go for a walk
4. go to the movies or stay at home
5. and the door will open
6. or you will(you'll) miss the train

03 p.103

1. Samantha has many caps and hats.
   and: 그리고, ~와
2. Would you like to pay in cash or by card?
   or: 또는, 아니면
3. Tom can speak English, but he can't speak Korean.
   but: 그러나, 하지만
4. He spoke loudly, so everyone could hear him well.
   so: 그래서, 그러므로

5. Do it right now, or you will not finish it.
명령문+or: ~해라, 그렇지 않으면

6. Study hard, and you can get a good grade.
명령문+and: ~해라, 그러면

통합서술형

(1) Sally and I will go to the movies tomorrow.
(2) I like action movies, but Sally doesn't (like action movies).
(3) Which do you like better, action movies or horror movies?
(4) Call me, and we can talk more about this.

해석 | 안녕, David. 나 Clara야. Sally와 나는 내일 영화 보러 갈 거야. 너도 같이 갈래? 나는 액션 영화를 좋아하지만 Sally는 좋아하지 않아. 그녀는 공포 영화를 좋아해. 넌 액션 영화와 공포 영화 중 어떤 것을 더 좋아하니? 내게 전화해, 그러면 이에 대해 더 얘기할 수 있을 거야.

CORE 29 명사절을 이끄는 접속사 that

Grammar Check 1 p.104

1. 주어 2. 보어 3. 목적어 4. 주어

Grammar Check 2

1. I think √ you and your brother are very kind.
2. The point is √ we don't have enough time.
3. It is certain √ he will come back home tomorrow.
4. The problem is √ I don't know his phone number.

01 p.105

1. that she'll become a history teacher
2. that he arrived there on time
3. that Dick will go to Seoul tomorrow
4. is possible that Max finishes the work in 2 hours
5. that Dave will pass the entrance exam

02

1. I think that you are
2. My hope is that I can swim
3. It is certain that Steve will go
4. The good news is that he won
5. It is surprising that she can speak

03 p.106

1. said (that) I had a cold
2. thinks (that) the story is fun
3. is true that she got an A
4. is that I'll be a teacher

통합서술형

(1) Today I learned that Madame Curie discovered radium.
(2) It is surprising that Madame Curie studied hard under hard conditions.

CORE 30 부사절을 이끄는 접속사

Grammar Check p.107

1. before 2. if 3. Unless
4. because 5. Because of

01 p.108

1. when 2. because(as/since) 3. If
4. Before 5. while 6. Unless

02

1. after 2. Because(As/Since)
3. unless 4. If 5. because of

03 p.109

1. because(as/since) I was tired
2. if you need my help
3. While my mother was out
4. unless you are busy(if you are not busy)
5. before you take a trip

통합서술형

after, before, unless, so, while

해석 | 나는 아침 7시 30분에 일어났다. 나는 아침을 먹은 후 학교에 갔다. 집으로 돌아오기 전에 나는 Kevin을 만났다. 비가 오지 않는다면 우리는 일요일에 스키를 타러 갈 것이다. 나는 내일 시험이 있으므로 수학 공부를 했다. 나는 지금 음악을 들으면서 일기를 쓰고 있다.

중학영어 **문법+쓰기**

- ▶ 중학영어 필수 문법을 엄선하여 정리하였습니다.
- ▶ 문법 포인트를 활용한 체계적인 3단계 쓰기 훈련과 통합 서술형 문제를 통해 중학영어 문법과 쓰기를 마스터 합니다.